Heterosexual Women Changing the Family

Feminist Perspectives on The Past and Present
Advisory Editorial Board

Heterosexual Women Changing the Family

Refusing to be a 'Wife'!

Jo VanEvery
Keele University

Taylor & Francis
Publishers since 1798

UK   Taylor & Francis Ltd, 4 John St., London WC1N 2ET
USA   Taylor & Francis Inc., 1900 Frost Road, Suite 101, Bristol, PA 19007

First published 1995

**Library Catalogue Record for this book is available from the British
Library**

ISBN 0 7484 0283 7
ISBN 0 7484 0284 5 (pbk)

**Library of Congress Cataloging-in-Publication Data are available
on request**

Series cover design by Amanda Barragry.

Typeset in 11/13pt Times by Solidus (Bristol) Limited

*Printed in Great Britain by Biddles Ltd, Guildford and King's Lynn on
paper which has a specified pH value on final paper manufacture of not
less than 7.5 and is therefore 'acid free'.*

For Tara and Joh who introduced me
to the possibility of living differently

Contents

List of Tables

Preface and Acknowledgments

This book addresses two audiences. On the one hand, I embarked on this research motivated by a personal desire to know more about the ways that women were putting feminist ideals into practice in their personal and domestic lives. In part, I wanted to provide a resource for other women, like myself, who wanted to make use of the experience of others in their attempts at non-oppressive living. Because I chose to do this research in the context of a higher degree in sociology, I wanted (and needed) to address some sociological questions. I have tried to do this in a way that does not make my research inaccessible to the non-academic reader. To this end, there is only a brief discussion of the methods used in the main text. For those who are interested a more detailed treatment of these issues can be found in an appendix. I have also tried to present the information gained in the interviews in a way which both contributes to my analysis and provides information for other women about the details of these living arrangements. This detail is often summarized in tables.

I would like to thank the following people for their part in making this book possible. I am sure to have left someone out but the process of research and writing is dependent on so many that this may be inevitable. I apologize for any omissions. Linda Cardinal encouraged me to pursue postgraduate study. Mary McIntosh agreed to supervise the project and provided initial encouragement, some of the supervision and advice. Lydia Morris took over the supervision of the project when Mary went on leave. Her attention to detail and commitment to the task was invaluable. Suzanne Desaulniers, and Marion Coleman and Jana Walters have allowed me to use unpublished material. Mary Girling, Brenda Corti, and the secretaries in the Department of Sociology have provided assistance on numerous occasions. The staff and students in the Essex University Sociology Department provided a supportive environment in which much of the work was done. Thanks, also, to Comfort Jegede at Taylor & Francis for encouraging me to turn the thesis into a book and an anonymous reader for some helpful suggestions.

Financial assistance was provided by my parents, John and Barbara VanEvery; my godmother, the late Johanna Murray; the Committee of Vice-Chancellors and Principals, in the form of an Overseas Students Award; and the University of Essex, Department of Sociology Fuller Fund, in the form of assistance with travel expenses. I would also like to thank the *Guardian* Women's Page for including the appeal for participants in their Bulletin.

I would especially like to thank my friends for their encouragement, long discussions, book references (and loans), and emotional, practical and political support. In particular, Joanne Springthorpe, Becky Nixon, Mat Paterson, Mark Rogers, Nikki Craske and Pingla Udit. For the original inspiration and my desire to create an alternative family, I thank Tara Jones and Johanne Bérubé who once shared meals, drudgery, laughter and tears. Last but not least, I thank all those who participated in the study (and the many more who responded but were not included) without whom there would be no book.

Chapter 1

Family and Women's Oppression

In September 1982, at the age of 18, I left Nova Scotia to attend the University of Ottawa. In my first year I shared a room in the halls of residence. I remember talking to my roommate about our plans for the future, and her characterization of mine as 'little girls' dreams'. I had accepted my mother's values and, although I sought a university degree, expected to get married, have children and give up my career/job in order to raise those children.

During the course of my undergraduate studies, I took a year out and changed courses from chemistry to sociology. I took some courses on women and gender inequalities, and began to read feminist analyses of society. Like many other women who became interested in feminism, I began to question the character of my personal relationships. By this time I was sharing a flat with two other women. We ate an evening meal together and split the housework in an informal but equal way. We were friends but our close emotional relationships were not limited to the residential group. I felt that I would like to live in this sort of arrangement in the long term but I realized that the other two women saw it as a temporary arrangement while we were at university. We all knew that one day we would 'grow up, get married and have kids' even if we now expected to have careers as well.

I was aware that it was not just the personal views of these two women which prevented me from choosing this type of living arrangement on a permanent basis. These were generally accepted beliefs. Despite the fact that at any given time households comprising married couples with children under 16 years of age form a minority of all households, most people live in them for significant portions of their lives both as children and as adults, and (perhaps more importantly) expect to do so.

I looked to the feminist literature for an analysis of, and perhaps an answer to, this very personal dilemma. The feminist literature is rife with criticisms of 'the family' and its various component parts (e.g. the isolated nature of the nuclear family household, compulsory heterosexuality, the division of domestic labour, mothering). The issue of alternatives to 'the family' is raised briefly in many feminist writings but is usually anecdotal (see e.g. Segal, 1983). Although older[1] feminists who have tried alternative living arrangements often suggest reasons for their failure —

> Among the most acute and time-consuming [difficulties and contra-dictions] were probably those which arose from the lack of rules and criteria available to help negotiate the new contexts in which traditional relations, expectations and modes of behaviour had been called into question.
>
> (Nava, 1983, p. 76)

— these seem to be based solely on their own attempts to understand their own experiences. There has been no systematic study of feminist alternatives.

As a woman who came to feminism in the mid-1980s, I became aware of a life-cycle effect in both British and American feminist writing which is particularly evident in the area of alternative living arrangements.

> We have tried being independent without children, we have used nurseries, even instituted non-sexist ones. Fought hard to remove sexual divisions in the home. Turned ourselves inside out in efforts to shed ideologies of the family, monogamy, jealousy, romantic love and dependence.
>
> Implicit in all our strivings of the last years has been an adaption to the world of work, rather than the adaption of that world to one that allows time for children, leisure, politics ...
>
> ... What are the demands about work which would assimilate domestic experience? What kinds of demands, or ways of thinking about demands, would express the concrete and complex reality of most women, which includes waged work and domestic life and children?
>
> (Campbell and Charlton, 1978, quoted in Rowbotham, 1989a, p. 31)

Similar arguments are commonly used in feminist discussions of political strategies. But by framing demands for changes in the public sphere in this way, those of us who have not tried the things mentioned in the first paragraph are excluded. Our questions are not addressed. Younger feminists are left with a critique of 'the family', which is still what we are expected to form (by our parents, friends, the state and others), but a lack of options to replace it with.

I was not convinced that no one tried to institute political change in their personal lives any more so I decided to undertake a systematic study of those who did. My interest in feminism narrowed my field of interest from alternative families to living arrangements which were specifically anti-sexist. I was interested in the ways that women went about trying to put feminist principles into practice in their personal lives, and the problems and successes that they had had. I hoped that this information would be useful to other women like myself (and those in the study) who were trying to find non-oppressive ways of living.

By this time I had spent a year as an exchange student in England. I had met academics who were interested in my question and decided to stay in England to conduct the research.[2] The study was relatively small; I interviewed members of 26 living arrangements and information about two more was included in the analysis. Of those only three women (from two living arrangements) were identified as lesbian. Many of the living arrangements included were organized around a heterosexual couple. In what follows I examine the strategies of these heterosexual women. I do not wish to diminish in any way the significance for feminism of lesbian strategies. However, many women have rejected these strategies for various reasons. In this book I explore the possibilities which remain open to them.

Doing the Research

When I embarked on this research, my main interest was in exploring how women translated the feminist critique of the family into practice. For example, what kinds of living arrangements did they form? How did they divide the work that needed to be done? I had read some material on feminist research methods and felt that a small qualitative study would be the best way to examine this question. The major advantage of qualitative research was that it would allow the participants the scope to define the important issues.

It has been suggested to me, however, that such a small group of uncommon living arrangements cannot tell us much about gender and families. I would argue that this is not the case. It is increasingly recognized within sociology that power relationships are often invisible (and indeed may depend for their effectiveness on their invisibility). They become visible only on the breakdown of or other disruption to the relationships. So, for example, Carol Smart has studied divorce in order to learn more about marriage (Smart, 1984). The members of the living arrangements I have studied are consciously trying to counter oppressive relationships. Through the study of these anti-sexist living arrangements, various aspects of our society become visible: the character of 'normal' families, the interaction between the public and private spheres, and the gendered character of many (all?) social roles, identities and locations. As regards the size of the sample, Dorothy Smith has pointed out that any story (such as the stories participants told me about their living arrangements) bears traces of the social relations in which it is embedded (Smith, 1990, p. 217). Qualitative research done on a small scale allows for attention to the details of these stories at various levels.

The details of the methods used and the principles of feminist methodology are outlined in Appendix 2. Here, I will summarize how I went about the research and the main characteristics of the participants. A brief description of each living arrangement is given in Appendix 1 and numbers in square brackets in the text assist the reader to cross-reference the main discussion to this list. The participants identified themselves to me in response to advertisements in feminist media and notices in the newsletters of organizations such as the Working Mothers Association (now Parents At Work). Based on information contained in their letters, I chose 26 living arrangements for interview, about equally divided amongst the following five categories: single mothers by choice, voluntarily childless heterosexual couples, heterosexual couples with children in role reversals, heterosexual couples with children with shared roles, and multiple adult living arrangements (with or without children). There were a few which I grouped separately as 'others' including a voluntarily childless single woman, a heterosexual couple who did not live together and a lesbian couple. The book focuses on heterosexual women's strategies because only the lesbian couple and one of the single mothers identified themselves as lesbian.[3] I will, however, use some of the material from their interviews for illustrative purposes.

Geographically, participants came from a variety of (mainly urban) locations in Britain. Two living arrangements were in Scotland; the rest were in England. All the participants were white. Most would be considered middle class particularly in terms of their occupations. However, incomes ranged from Income Support to over £200 000 per annum. Some participants were from working-class backgrounds. Most were well educated, many having degrees or other post-secondary qualifications and some having postgraduate degrees. Although these characteristics could be said to limit the applicability of the findings, the participants could also be described as having a better than average chance of being able to exert control over their personal lives. Any constraints on their ability to change would reflect not factors such as poverty or racism but, rather, the resistance of particular constructions of gender and family to change.

Interviews were conducted in 1991 (most in the summer) and usually took place in the homes of the participants, and lasted about 90 minutes on average. I began by briefly stating the aims of the research and asking them to speak about their living arrangement. I had a list of topics that I wanted to cover and asked questions when necessary. This format allowed a certain amount of freedom to the participants while allowing me to set some boundaries within which all of the interviews would fit. The interviews were analysed using an interpretive method. Information on specific themes which I identified as important was then systematically organized and analysed.

In order to make sense of this material, I made use of feminist and sociological theories. In this chapter I will outline the theoretical principles that guide the analysis reported in the rest of the book. The theoretical framework set out here was developed in the process of analysing the interview material. During the analysis, I went back and forth between the 'data' and various theories trying to make sense of what I had. None of the theories was wholly adequate to the task but I believe that I have brought them together in a coherent manner.

The initial questions guiding my research were broad. In part, this was to allow the participants' concerns to focus the research. In the process of analysis, the guiding question was refined. This book sets out to answer the question 'What is an anti-sexist living arrangement?' The short answer is in the title – refusing to be a wife.

Gender and the Family in 'Standard Sociological Theory'

Talcott Parsons's theory of the family has been so influential that David Cheal has called it the 'Standard Theory of the Family' (1991, p. 3). A discussion of his work highlights some of the issues considered important in the sociological research on families and households. Parsons argues that the modern family is a relatively isolated, small unit specializing in the functions of socialization of children and personality stabilization of adults (Parsons and Bales, 1955, p. 16). This unit is commonly referred to in social science research as the nuclear family household and consists of a married heterosexual couple and their own children. Parsons theorizes family as one system within a set of hierarchically organized systems and subsystems in a society which evolves by the criterion of 'enhancement of adaptive capacity' (Cheal, 1991, p. 32). Basically, as society evolves the division of labour becomes more specialized and adaptation is necessary.

The most well-known aspect of Parsons's work on the family — the division between expressive and instrumental roles — is seen as an enhancement of adaptive capacity necessary to industrialization. The increased specialization of roles includes a split between the public and the private spheres as well as a gender dimension. The gender specialization of instrumental and expressive tasks is paralleled by the separation of work and home. The structural isolation of the nuclear family from the wider kin group is organized to free the man in the instrumental role for geographical mobility which may be demanded by the occupational system. Men go out to work and provide for the family, women stay in the home performing their expressive roles. The two roles have been seen as incompatible and the instrumental nature of much of women's role has been played down even when recognized.

Parsons's explanation of the assignment of roles by gender is based on the biological fact of childbirth.

> In our opinion the fundamental explanation of the allocation of the roles between the biological sexes lies in the fact that the bearing and early nursing of children establish a strong presumptive primacy of the relation of mother to the small child and this in turn establishes a presumption that the man, who is exempted from these biological functions, should specialize in the alternative instrumental direction.
>
> (Parsons and Bales, 1955, p. 23)

The separation of public from private and the relative isolation of the nuclear family household increases the differentiation of sex roles.[4] His theory of 'the family' is, thus, also a theory of gender.

Although Parsons's analysis of the family is often seen to indicate a complementarity of roles and he has been criticized for ignoring power relationships within the family, he does construe the man as head of the household: to compensate for the loss of responsibility in the labour market, the worker's 'organizational responsibility for the security and prestige of his household is paramount' (Parsons and Smelser, 1956, pp. 147–8). Parsonian theory also recognizes that women's role was not always a particularly enjoyable one (see Harris, 1983, p. 61) but, one assumes owing to his beliefs about the nature of social science, his purpose remained to describe and explain the existing structure of society. More recent work in this tradition, both feminist and non-feminist, attempts to explain the rise in divorce and single motherhood as a consequence of women's entry into the labour market (e.g. Johnson, 1989; Popenoe, 1988).

In Britain, Marxist theory was also influential. Women on the left who were also involved in the women's movement made strenuous efforts both to find a Marxian analysis of women's position in society and the family and, when that failed, to create one. This focused mainly on the relationship between domestic and non-domestic labour and will be discussed in more detail in Chapter 3. However, Marx wrote little about women and the family and there is no systematic analysis of gender divisions in society in his work.

What was written in this tradition suffered from many of the same problems as Parsonian theory. Both theories explained family in relation to the capitalist/modern industrial economy. Marx and Engels also conceived of the sexual division of labour as the 'natural' division of labour 'between man and woman for child-breeding' (quoted in Sydie, 1987, p. 90). They did not see this division of labour as inherently unequal but explained inequality through the importance attributed in capitalist society to productive labour and private property. What is useful about both of these theoretical traditions is their approach to the family as a system of social relations. Both traditions also attempted to theorize the links between the private and the public spheres (albeit inadequately).

Feminist Critiques

Feminist critiques of the standard sociological position can be said to focus on the two central organizing principles: the separation of instrumental and expressive tasks (or, in relation to Marxist theory, productive and reproductive labour), including the definitions of each type; and the division between the public and the private, including the way that this division is said to mirror the first one. In both cases the gendering of the dichotomies is made central.

Following from Betty Friedan's (1963) exposure of the 'role strain' experienced by white middle-class women, feminists focused on the instrumental nature of much of women's work in the home. There was a process of naming the things that housewives did as 'work', including the work involved in mothering and child-care, from changing dirty nappies to supervising homework. More recent studies have highlighted the nature of more narrowly defined 'expressive' tasks as work; and Arlie Hochschild has been especially influential in the theorization of 'emotion work' (1983, 1990). Others have pointed out the work involved in 'kin keeping' activities — writing letters, remembering birthdays, etc. — essential to maintaining support networks and usually performed by women (Finch, 1989, pp. 40, 71; Leonardo, 1987, pp. 442–3). Within the Marxist tradition, criticism has focused on the 'productive' aspects of housework and mothering (e.g. Delphy and Leonard, 1992, pp. 80–3).

The feminist critique of the assumed separation of the public and private spheres is indicated in the slogan 'the personal is political'. Kate Millett (1971) was one of the first to point out that 'the political' was not conterminous with 'the public'. Feminist political scientists have concentrated on this use of the dichotomy producing cogent critiques of liberal political

7

thought (see Pateman, 1983). Another crucial component of the feminist critique of the public/private dichotomy is its basis in the 'natural'. As noted above, both Parsons, and Marx and Engels based the gender division of labour on women's unique ability to bear children. R. A. Sydie (1987), among others, has demonstrated that the nature/culture dichotomy underlies most 'classical' sociological thought.

Within sociology, the public/private dichotomy has been addressed primarily in terms of the housework/paid work distinction. The key issue is the allocation of the gendered roles that sociologists identified to two different spheres. Feminists challenged the separation of the two and the necessity of housework and child-care being done in private (e.g. Benston, 1969; Rowbotham, 1972), stressing the social character of the activities heretofore termed 'natural'. Whilst emphasizing the socially constructed nature of gender roles, feminists have also drawn attention to the fact that women are disadvantaged in employment and this disadvantage is related to their domestic situation (see Beechey, 1988; Witz, 1993). Involvement in work in the public sphere assumes that one's private needs are taken care of (e.g. Acker, 1990, p. 149; Finch, 1983), and labour market opportunities for women may assume a domestic commitment (e.g. Beechey and Perkins, 1985). Marriage and mothering are in many ways 'rational' choices given the economic structure of society (Barrett and McIntosh, 1982, pp. 21, 75; Delphy and Leonard, 1992).

As well as the gendered division of labour, one major area of concern for feminists studying the family has been the way that 'the socialization of children' has been gender socialization. Psychoanalysis has been used extensively to try to understand the roots of misogyny and sexism in childhood (e.g. Chodorow, 1978). However, there is another branch of feminist theorizing which has analysed the way that adult relationships within the family construct gender. Because these feminists do not call the object of their critique 'the family', their insights have been overlooked or marginalized in this area.

Radical lesbian feminists have developed a cogent critique of heterosexuality as a practice and institution which constructs gender. The essence of this critique is that gender is constructed as a power relationship with men as dominators and women as subordinates. In developing this critique they have focused mainly on actual sexual practices (mainly fucking). Some radical lesbian feminists, in making an argument for separatism as a political practice, expand this to discuss heterosexuality in a much broader sense thus linking heterosexism (the assumption that individuals are heterosexual) with sexism. It is this broader sense of heterosexuality which I will use in my application of this critical perspective to 'the family', which includes a heterosexual couple.

Gender as Social Construction

To say that gender is socially constructed does not mean that it is superficial or 'not real'. It is, rather, to say that it is not inevitable or inevitably the way it is now, though it may be very difficult to change. In our society, gender is constructed in a way that refers to biological characteristics which 'are used to reinforce the "essentialness" of gender' (West and Zimmerman, 1987, p. 137). Thus biological differences in hormone levels, genetic structures, and bodily characteristics are said to differ systematically in such a way that two, and only two, sex categories exist.[5] Differences which do not fit into these two categories are classified as 'problems' and corrected. Social differences between these two categories can then be explained (at least partly) with reference to these biological differences.

Candace West and Don Zimmerman (1987) argue further that gender is always relevant in social interaction. Marilyn Frye (1983a) uses the example of the anxiety experienced when we cannot identify someone's gender to illustrate the same point. West and Zimmerman use the notion of 'accountability' to understand the way that gender affects all social interaction.

> ... a person engaged in virtually any activity may be held accountable for performance of that activity as a *woman* or a *man*, and their incumbency in one or the other sex category can be used to legitimate or discredit their other activities.... to 'do' gender is not always to live up to normative conceptions of femininity or masculinity; it is to engage in behaviour *at the risk of gender assessment.*
>
> (1987, p. 136; original emphasis)

An example from Scott Coltrane's research on men who share child-care illustrates this process. He found that it was important to be seen as a breadwinner if a man shared child-care and housework because if one is a breadwinner one can be seen as a man (1989, p. 488). Furthermore, many of the men did not tell their colleagues that they were heavily involved in child-care as it was a discredited activity for *men* to engage in.

Although I find West and Zimmerman's conceptualization useful, it lacks one key component. As Hester Eisenstein (1991, p. 111) says, 'Theories of gender are fundamentally about relations of domination and subordination and about how these are perpetuated or contested'. This has been perhaps the most important point about radical lesbian separatist critiques of heterosexuality — it is not about complementarity but domination (see e.g. Frye, 1983a). Linking this to the observation that all social relations are gendered,

leads to a perspective on family relationships which sees them as constructing and reconstructing ('doing') gender.

Anti-sexist Living Arrangements

As Hester Eisenstein (1991, p. 88) points out, feminists have tended not to look
at 'the family' but rather have focused on its component parts. When 'the
family' has been discussed it is often as an ideological construction which
regulates women's lives (e.g. Barrett and McIntosh, 1982). The sociological
study of families has also changed in recognition of increasing diversity. The
question 'What is the family?' took three sentences to answer in one 1960
textbook (Bell and Vogel, 1960, p. 1) but by 1986 Faith Robertson Elliot
devotes four pages to it (Elliot, 1986, pp. 4–8). Jeffrey Weeks points out that this
move towards definitions which are inclusive of diverse forms of intimate
relationships 'must be seen as a political response to diversity rather than a
useful sociological categorisation' (1991, p. 227). Michèle Barrett and Mary
McIntosh emphasize that this still leaves some people outside of 'family' and
thus unable to access its benefits (1982, esp. pp. 76–80).

In order to overcome the problems identified with the term 'family',
some scholars prefer to use household as the basis for their research and
problematize the relationships within households.[6] However, even a cursory
glance at the literature on housework, financial allocation in households, etc.
will reveal that the most common form of household studied is composed of
a married couple with children under 16. Minor variations on this model are
sometimes found but marriage (or marriage-like relationships) seems to be
the focus of this research.

The household is a residential arrangement but involves more than
co-residence:

> ... households might be characterised by a shared set of activities
> such as sleeping, food preparation, eating, sexual relations, and
> caring for those who cannot care for themselves.
>
> (Gittens, 1993, p. 61)

As Diana Gittens (1993) notes, there are still problems with this definition
and my research raises some of these. In particular, the idea of the 'common
pot' often used by census enumerators to distinguish households from other
co-resident groups is questioned by those in my study who normally do not
eat together.[7] The concept of the household has also been criticized for its
implicit assumption of equality and consensus within the unit, notably in the

study of domestic violence and child abuse but also in the study of the economics of the household (e.g. J. Pahl, 1980).

Definitions are contested precisely because of their political character (Barrett and McIntosh, 1982; Weeks, 1991). Jeffrey Weeks differentiates between 'diversity' and 'alternatives'. While 'diversity' is inclusive of a variety of forms that 'family' might take, it implies an acceptance of 'family' as a desirable unit. In contrast, 'alternatives' imply a critique of the family (however that might be defined or understood) and the necessity of finding better ways of meeting our emotional and developmental needs. Most studies take structural criteria as the basis for their definitions, leading to a plethora of possible alternatives depending on the definition of the structural norm assumed.[8] However, I have opted for a political criterion and focus specifically on *anti-sexist* alternatives. I return to Frye for a definition:

> The term 'sexist' characterizes cultural and economic structures which create and enforce the elaborate and rigid patterns of sex-marking and sex-announcing which divide the species, along lines of sex, into dominators and subordinates. Individual acts and practices are sexist which reinforce and support those structures, either as culture or as shapes taken on by the enculturated animals. Resistance to sexism [or anti-sexism] is that which undermines those structures by social and political action and by projects of reconstruction and revision of ourselves.
>
> (1983a, p. 38)

A common misconception of my project is that I am studying *non*-sexist alternatives. Given the omnirelevance of sex category (to use West and Zimmerman's phrase), I do not believe non-sexist behaviour is possible. My focus is on those with a political critique of women's position in society who are pursuing change at a 'personal' level by trying to create anti-sexist living arrangements. This may involve a redefinition of roles, a different household structure, or both.

I have used the term 'living arrangement' in an attempt to overcome the problematic assumptions of both 'family' and 'household'. This term retains the scope for self-definition in terms of who is included (within or beyond household boundaries) and what the relationships between members are. There were also situations where I needed a replacement for the term 'household' and have opted for the term 'residential group'. Both 'family' and 'household' are commonly used in everyday conversation and in sociological and feminist literature. The terms will thus appear occasionally throughout the book.

Analysing the Data

When people talk about families, they talk about personal relationships, housework, love, going out to work, etc. No one told me explicitly what they meant by an anti-sexist living arrangement though some told my why they had responded to my advertisement. As Marjorie DeVault (1990) has pointed out it is important to listen for the things that are difficult to articulate in our interviews. I have had to answer my question, 'What is an anti-sexist living arrangement?', by looking at the way that participants talked about the various practices and relationships that made up their lives. I identified three important themes in the interview material — housework, mothering and non-domestic work. Analysis of these themes often indicated other related or subsidiary themes. An explanation of my choice of terms will allow me to explain the theoretical material that informs my analysis. The themes themselves form the basis of the following chapters.

As noted earlier, feminists have been critical of the use of the term 'work' to apply only to productive, remunerated labour in the public sphere and have been largely successful in expanding its usage in sociological research. However, as Christine Delphy and Diana Leonard (1992) have pointed out, different kinds of work are organized in different social relations. I have chosen the term 'non-domestic work' over the more commonly used phrases 'paid work' and 'work outside the home' to refer to that work which is not 'of the home' (*Oxford Concise English Dictionary*).[9]

The more common terms rest on an assumption of a division between public and private and an allocation of remunerated, productive work to one sphere and housework and child-care to the other. This is especially true of the phrase 'work outside the home'. The phrase 'paid work' cannot encompass activities which may be unpaid but non-domestic. These include voluntary work, political activism and work which may in some cases be remunerative but not always. The third possibility is illustrated by two of the women participants who stated that they had careers as writers even though they had no offers from publishers and therefore no money coming in for their writing.

I have also decided to refer to domestic work as 'housework'.[10] My view of feminist research as explaining society for women prioritizes the use of language women understand and use. Eva Kaluzynska (1980) notes that 'housework' became 'domestic labour' when Marxists started to theorize about it and that the 'Domestic Labour Debate' was addressed to Marxists rather than women (1980, p. 40). Despite the intentions of the authors who contributed to this debate, the language and place of publication was generally inaccessible to the mass of women. 'The writings on housework

that made the most lingering impact on the movement called housework housework, rather than domestic labour' (Kaluzynska, 1980, p. 51).
Although I recognize the importance of using the term 'labour' within the
theoretical traditions of Marxism, I am not convinced of its necessity as a
prerequisite for the recognition of the importance of housework.

Child-care is often excluded from the definition of housework (e.g.
Oakley, 1974a) and its inclusion is often used as an argument in favour of
the term 'domestic labour'. This practice seems to be based on the
assumption that common usage of the term 'housework' does not include
child-care. I remain unconvinced that this is the case.[11] Delphy and Leonard
(1992) address the issue of defining housework in some detail. They argue
against the definition of the term as a list of tasks because the tasks which
may be involved are variable (not only historically and culturally, but also
individually). I find their definition of 'housework' — 'the composite of
regular day-to-day tasks which are judged necessary to maintain a home'
(1992, p. 99) — useful as it allows some scope for self-definition of the
precise tasks involved.[12] The discussion of housework in the interviews was
very general and allowed the participants to talk about the tasks that they felt
were relevant. In the analysis, I grouped tasks in ways that made sense of the
divisions practised in the living arrangements studied. I considered child-care
as a category of housework.

However, I also found that Miriam Johnson's (1988) work on mothers
and wives provided a useful way of looking at women's domestic lives. She
argues that it is important to separate the roles of mother and wife
analytically in order to understand the oppression of women. I will use the
term 'mothering' to refer to the set of activities, emotions and relationships
involved in raising children. I have chosen the term 'mothering' despite its
gender-specific connotations. Mothering is undertaken primarily by women
in most known societies although it is not always limited to the biological
mother of the child. Mothering could (to a great extent) be done by men but
generally is not. Mothering is undervalued in society and men, for the most
part, do not mother (or when they do it is often under the influence of or
pressure from women).[13] I have also chosen to refer to mothers as women
except when I specifically refer to the experiences of men.

Understanding the Oppression of Women

In her book *Strong Mothers, Weak Wives* Miriam Johnson (1988) locates
women's oppression in the role of wife which is by definition subordinate
and under which the role of mother has been subsumed. Christine Delphy and

Jo VanEvery

Diana Leonard's (1992) theory of the economic nature of male power in the family household provides a deeper understanding of the content of the role of wife (as the structural position in which women are located) and the way that it subsumes mothering within it.

Delphy and Leonard's analysis also extends our understanding of women's position in non-domestic work by showing how the role of wife also exists in this sphere. Carole Pateman provides a more detailed understanding of this position, pointing out the gendered nature of both the public and the private spheres. In particular, Pateman is critical of the concept of the individual which, despite its apparent gender neutrality, is a masculine notion.

Pateman also emphasizes that the organization of the public sphere is dependent on particular kinds of work being done in the private sphere. The two are thus mutually dependent. Joan Acker specifies the way that organizations are structured to reproduce this dependence on an individual level.

> In organizational logic, both jobs and hierarchies are abstract categories that have no occupants, no human bodies, no gender. However, an abstract job can exist, can be transformed into a concrete instance, only if there is a worker. In organizational logic, filling the abstract job is a disembodied worker who exists only for the work. Such a hypothetical worker cannot have other imperatives of existence that impinge upon the job. At the very least, outside imperatives cannot be included within the definition of the job. Too many obligations outside the boundaries of the job would make a worker unsuited for the position. The closest the disembodied worker doing the abstract job comes to a real worker is the male worker whose life centers on his full-time, life-long job, while his wife or another woman takes care of his personal needs and his children.
>
> (Acker, 1990, p. 149)

Together these theories provide a framework in which we can understand the part played by the family in the oppression of women. Structurally, it resembles the Parsonian model but complementarity has been replaced by relationships of domination and subordination. Women are wives; men are workers. The two are in a relationship of mutual dependence which forms the basis of unequal power relationships. The role of mother is subsumed under that of wife. But these are not only 'roles' or structural positions. Forms of personal identity are linked to them. For example, being a mother is an important part of many women's identities. For this reason, I have used the compound term role/identity in this book. By doing so I hope to indicate both the structural and personal aspects of being a wife, mother or worker.

Within the theoretical framework I am developing 'wife' is not defined simply as 'a married woman' (*Oxford Concise English Dictionary*) although most such women would come within its scope. Rather, it refers to the particular social position of women as subordinates of individual men. For Johnson (1988) the characteristics central to the definition of 'wife' are subordinate status and economic dependence. Delphy and Leonard (1992) specify the economic characteristics of wife further to include the appropriation of labour, paid and unpaid, by the (male) head of household, including the work involved in raising his children as well as any work done for someone else.[14]

Carole Pateman's (1988) work on the 'sexual contract' which underlies the 'social contract' of liberal individualism highlights the fact that husbands' rights still include the right to their wives' work and sexual rights, and that relations between men and women include the right of male access to female bodies.[15] Johnson notes the elision of sexuality and gender in our society, heterosexuality being the basis of the definition of femininity and masculinity. Thus being a 'wife' includes a characteristic sexual component.

Although the separation of wife, mother and worker is useful analytically, we must remember that they are not usually separated in practice. The three roles/identities interact and intertwine in various ways. Some of these are indicated by the theorists to whom I refer. The elision of mothering with the other duties of a wife is evident in Ann Oakley's work. Delphy and Leonard theorize the labour involved as part of the total unpaid labour appropriated by the head of household. Johnson highlights the way that maternal values of relationality and interdependence are counteracted by 'wifely' characteristics of deference and subordination.

Because my analysis takes the domestic as the point of entry from which to explore gender relations, I have focused on the way that wives and mothers appear in the private sphere. However, as Carole Pateman and others have pointed out, the public/private split is largely a fiction. Workers appear in the private sphere as breadwinners. Cynthia Cockburn's (1991) analysis of the way that men resist equal opportunities in the workplace highlights the way that men actively place women in the role of wife in the public sphere. This is especially evident in the sexualization of women and resistance to women in authority. Delphy and Leonard (1992) point out that the social role of wife appears in the occupational sphere both in the types of segregated work women perform (e.g. secretaries, waitresses) and in the expectations of certain professional jobs. In addition, women's ability to undertake non-domestic work is controlled by the male head of household either directly, through the giving or withholding of permission, or indirectly, through the expectation that non-domestic work cannot affect the performance of domestic duties.

There are various ways that women can resist and reject the role/identity of wife. The first group of tactics comprises the formal aspects of that role: marriage, taking the man's name, having a head of household. Second, one must consider rejection of and resistance to the economic aspects of wife identified by Delphy and Leonard: economic dependence and the appropriation of potentially all their labour. Third, there is resistance to and rejection of the appropriation of emotional and sexual labour (or control of sexuality). One might also see this resistance reflected in attempts to redefine both mothering and the importance of non-domestic work for women.

Notes

1   I use the adjectives 'older' and 'younger' to distinguish how long one has been involved in feminist politics, especially whether one was a feminist in the heyday of the 1970s.
2   The research reported in this book was conducted for a PhD in Sociology at the University of Essex under the supervision of Dr Lydia Morris and Dr Mary McIntosh and submitted under the title 'Anti-sexist Living Arrangements: A Feminist Research Project'. The PhD was awarded in July 1994.
3   Heterosexuality is an unmarked category; thus it is unrealistic to expect women to identify themselves in this way. Some of the participants did. Others were living in heterosexual couples or spoke about heterosexual relationships. Not all women were in such relationships, a point which will be dealt with later in the book.
4   Although this is the term used in Parsons's work, given the criticism of it (see Lopata and Thorne, 1978) the point might be clearer if phrased as 'increases the differentiation of social roles by sex'.
5   While in the final stages of writing the thesis on which this book is based, a television programme was screened which provided a vivid illustration of the way geneticists actively construct two sexes from much more ambiguous biological evidence ('Cracking the Code: Birth, Sex and Death', BBC 2, 21 September 1993).
6   For example, McCulloch (1982) who provides an explanation of the benefits of this approach. See also Morris (1989).
7   For a critical overview of definitions of 'family', 'household' and 'kinship' see Gittens (1993), Ch. 3.
8   Thus, in her review of the literature in the 1970s, Eleanor Macklin states 'It is an enormous, actually impossible, task to summarize in one article all of the research on nontraditional family forms conducted in the past decade. This is especially true if "nontraditional" is defined as all living patterns other than legal, lifelong, sexually exclusive marriage between one man and one woman, with children, where the male is the primary provider and ultimate authority' (Macklin, 1980, p. 905).
9   This definition of 'domestic' is not equivalent to the inside the home/outside the home distinction as work could be *of* the home and still take place outside it (e.g. food shopping). There are still problems with this distinction particularly if applied

to agricultural production (Pahl, 1988, pp. 10–11; Delphy and Leonard, 1992, Ch. 8). However, given that my sample is primarily urban and that a distinction is commonly made in late twentieth-century British society between domestic and non-domestic work, I have found it useful in the analysis of my interview material.

10 Although it did not arise as a paid activity amongst the people that I interviewed, paid domestic work would be considered with unpaid domestic work. Although Delphy and Leonard (1992) argue that paid domestic work would have the same social relations as other waged work, there have been very few studies in this area and evidence such as that found in Hertz (1986) indicates that this may not be the case.

11 For example, in her study of housework Ann Oakley specifically excluded child-care although she analysed the relationship between the two types of work and their conflation by some women. The four case studies included in Ann Oakley's *Housewife* (1974b) illustrate the inclusion of some child-care tasks (i.e. nappy washing) in understandings of housework.

12 Although I agree that the fact that it is unpaid is central to the character of housework, I have decided not to make it central to my definition. Some women are paid to do housework in other women's homes. The relations which govern this work are not the same as those governing non-domestic work and are similar in many respects to those governing unpaid housework. See, for example, Cock (1981) and Gaitskell *et al.* (1984). A less theoretical discussion is found in Hertz (1986, Ch. 5).

13 The obvious gender-neutral alternative would be 'parenting'. Susan Peterson argues against the use of this term on four grounds: that it is ahistorical and lacks a material base; that the political strategy of changing language is relatively powerless to effect changes in material conditions and creates the false impression that material conditions have changed more than they actually have (this would also apply to the use of 'domestic labour' for 'housework'); on moral grounds, that the use of the word 'parenting' deprives those doing the day-to-day work (usually women) of credit; and that it may disguise anti-feminist motives and actions (Peterson, 1984, p. 63). She argues for the use of the term 'mothering' or, as a compromise, 'nurturing'.

14 Women who are not married to a man may also have their labour thus appropriated either by a resident man (e.g. father or brother) or a non-resident man (e.g. the father of their children). Regarding the appropriation of women's labour by non-resident men see Delphy and Leonard (1992, p. 127, fn 6).

15 Other writers, concentrating on sexuality and female friendship, have focused in a similar way on men's control of women. My conceptualization of 'wife' is as the opposite of Marilyn Frye's (1992) use of the term 'virgin' (to mean 'a free woman, one not betrothed, not married, not bound to, not possessed by any man') and Janice Raymond's (1991) use of 'loose woman'.

Chapter 2

Marriage

Before moving on to the analysis of housework, mothering and non-domestic work, I would like to address the issue of marriage and anti-sexist living arrangements. Marriage has been a topic of feminist theorizing and political activism for hundreds of years (Tuttle, 1986). Struggles in the eighteenth and nineteenth centuries around (married) women's property rights and their rights to practise crafts and join guilds are well documented. Olive Banks, in her history of the twentieth-century feminist movement in the USA and Britain, points out that women trade unionists fought against the imposition of marriage bars in white-collar employment (1981, p. 218). In addition, a large number of feminist activists in the late nineteenth and early twentieth centuries were spinsters and had *chosen* to remain unmarried.

> They made such a choice, either because they regarded marriage as
> a form of humiliating slavery and dependence upon men, or because
> they wanted to pursue a career and fulfill their potential in such a way
> which would not have been allowed to them by husbands.
>   (Jeffreys, 1985, p. 88)

While Sheila Jeffreys's work is mainly concerned with the theories and politics of sexuality, she notes that many campaigns, e.g. for women's employment and education, stemmed from a concern with the ability of spinsters to be independent. She refers to the work of Rosemary Auchmuty who found that Victorian feminism was shaped by the concerns and leadership of Victorian spinsters (Jeffreys, 1985, p. 86).

In this historical material, two approaches to marriage can be discerned. On the one hand, some women sought changes to laws and practices which contributed to the oppression of married women. This may have been in the area of property and employment rights, or in issues related to sex and childbirth. The other approach, which often addressed the same or similar issues, was to refuse marriage and argue for the right of any woman to do so, her right to earn a living, and the strategic value of such a refusal.

Two similar strands can be discerned in what has become known as 'second wave' feminism. Some feminists have campaigned for the improvement of women's position in marriage, through legal changes and campaigns for economic equality. Socialist feminists are among those tending to focus on the conditions of marriage. Their analyses have tended to talk about the family rather than marriage and, for the most part, do not separate being a wife from being a mother (e.g. Barrett and McIntosh, 1982; Segal, 1983). Sheila Rowbotham, in her history of British socialist feminist organizing, refers to the 'Why Be a Wife' campaign in the late 1970s which 'challenged legal dependence, the allocation of domestic work, private responsibility for child-care, and the isolation of couples' (1989a, p. 32).

The other strand is evident in campaigns around sexual violence and wife battering, conducted mainly by radical feminists. This work led to theorizing around both the legal and economic constraints of marriage, which prevented women escaping violence and legitimized rape and violence in marriage, and the organization of sexuality. Political strategies included a refusal of marriage (and all heterosexual relations). Radical feminists also stress the importance of lesbianism as a political strategy (see *Trouble and Strife*, 1993).

Again, the two are not distinct. Socialist feminists have been active around issues of sexual violence, and radical feminists have fought for employment rights. As in the 'first wave', most of the activists in both strands are unmarried (a great many of them lesbian[1]). It is not surprising, given this history, that the issue of marriage is relevant to a discussion of anti-sexist living arrangements, or that there is considerable variety in the relationships studied.

Within sociology there has been a tendency to focus on marriage and little attention has been paid to the women on its margins (Chandler, 1991, pp. 1–3). Joan Chandler (1991) points out that all women are affected by marriage whether married themselves or not. Based on ideas developed in research on navy wives who, despite being married, spent considerable amounts of time without resident husbands, she argues that some women are more married than others. Chandler applies her ideas to cohabiting, widowed and divorced women highlighting the differences and commonalities of 'women without husbands'. Tuula Gordon (1994) has explored similar issues in the case of single women. Neither Chandler nor Gordon deals explicitly with the issue of feminism in relation to these women, although they draw attention to the issues of women's independence, and the social constraints on it. I hope that my study will complement theirs by drawing out the importance to women's liberation of making the margin the centre (Gordon, 1994, p. 192).

The Participants

In the idealisation of the nuclear family there is a clear delineation: women are either married or they are not. In reality women not only have a variety of marital statuses, they also have a range of domestic and sexual relationships with men.

(Chandler, 1991, p. 2)

In this chapter I will discuss the relationship of the participants to marriage. The terminology available is limited and inadequate. For example, there are women who are single but live in collective households and others who are in long-term heterosexual couples but live alone. In addition, many women talked about previous or intended relationships and living arrangements in the interviews. The discussion which follows, therefore, has not been subdivided into categories. Instead I have tried to move from the issues raised by some women's practices into those of others. Related issues are also discussed in Chapter 4 in the context of the choice to mother. Throughout the book names of participants will be followed by a number in square brackets. This is to allow the reader to refer to the details of each living arrangement provided in Appendix 1.

Two women in the study (Kate [1] and Jane [4]) have never cohabited with a man. Both are single mothers by choice. Jane recalls never wanting to marry even as a little girl. When I asked Kate whether she had ever considered cohabiting, she responded:

Kate: No, no, no, [. . .]² even if there have been people who the idea of spending a lot of time in their company was pleasant, let me put it like that, in fact, [pause] that's probably one of the things that stops me going very far with it because I can't imagine living with somebody, now. [. . .] it'd be so disruptive of the way I like to live and I suppose I've got over . . . I mean [pause] there have been times, say after my mother died, after [my daughter]'s gone to university, that certainly I've kind of felt lonely for adult company in the house. But not *male* company 'cause . . . more like family company or friend company. [. . .]

And it's a lot easier. [laughs] I mean, I have noticed [pause] I mean I don't ... you know, whatever makes people happy that's fine for them but it just does amuse me that some of the women who will say, 'I don't know how you manage' will then give you a list of complaints about the man they live with or the difficulties of living with a man. They make me think, 'Well, you know, sounds pretty hard work to me'.

At the other end of the spectrum are three couples who tell me that they are married but do not elaborate on this (Carol and Patrick [14]; Rebecca and Jack [12]; Christiane and Wilhelm [11]). Two more couples expand slightly: Paula and Rob [17] say that their marriage is a 'partnership' and there is no 'head' of household; Liz and Steve [10] say you have to work out a 'fit' in a marriage. Lynne and Dave [21] make a similar statement about working out the best way to be a family and note further that this changes over time.

Linked to this view of marriage is the idea that it is possible to control the meaning and practice of one's *own* marriage. There was some recognition, usually gained through experience, that this was limited. Paula and Rob [17] remark that things should have changed more than they have and that it should not be so difficult to be a partnership in practice. Liz and Steve [10] recognize that not all men would do what Steve has done (role reversal). Ann [3], a single mother by choice, spoke of her former marriage (long before the children were born) and her belief that she could do things differently. She soon realized that this was not possible and that external factors influenced its meaning and character.

One way that some women challenged their subordination in marriage was to keep their own names: six women did so, and Lynne [21] said that although she didn't at the time, she would now. Of those six, only one said that it was for business reasons. Three reported that some relatives had difficulty with this, usually apparent in the way they addressed envelopes: Eric's [18] father wrote 'Eric Potter and Jean'; Ian's [7] parents wrote to Peg and Ian as 'Mr and Mrs'; Louise's [8] brother wrote using both her and Mark's full names but put 'married couple' in parentheses after them. Two of the six couples in this group (Karen and Pete [6]; Barbara and Juan [9]) routinely did not tell people they were married and did not wear rings. They both spoke of not wanting to be treated 'as a couple'.

Jo: Do you think the fact of legally being married makes a difference in your relationship?
Pete: I don't think it makes much of a difference to us. [Karen] didn't change her name when we got married, for instance.
Karen: No, I don't ever wear a ring and neither does he. And we

don't ... I think we don't act like married people in a lot of areas, don't we?

P: Yeah. Well, people are very prone to treating you as a couple.

K: Yes.

P: Once you open up to being married.

K: Yes. They tend to think of you as husband and wife instead of people.

J: So you find other people treat you differently if they know that you're married?

P and K: Yes.

K: They expect you to be more conventional if you say you're married so we often don't. [pause] Particularly with the wife. In certain situations she can get invisible if she's 'a wife'. Like with his colleagues. They don't really know how to talk to 'a wife'. So he always introduces me as me, not as his wife. Then they've got to deal with me. That is nice.

The use of 'married' and 'couple' interchangeably in both accounts alerts us to the fact that not marrying may not solve the problem of being treated 'as a wife'. Five couples cohabited and one was separated after cohabitation. Roseanne and John [5] felt that cohabiting was part of what was 'alternative' about their living arrangement in contrast with the expectation that a couple was married and the woman had taken her husband's name.

Of the cohabiting couples, two (Laura and Chris; Jackie and Julian) were in the urban collective [19] and one (Mary and Alex) were in the rural collective [23]. Mary was about to move out to live in a flat with her children because she needed to be 'mistress of her own domain'. It is unclear to what extent this is related to cohabiting and to what extent, to collective living. Those who lived in collectives could minimize being treated as a couple, particularly by the state. Since they did not 'fit the boxes', state agencies had difficulty determining on whom a woman should be dependent. The collective situation may also contribute to perceptions based on other factors.

But I do get upset sometimes because people who don't know us very well or people who should know better don't recognize our relationship as a couple. Whether that's something I do or whether it's the way we live I don't know but I find that quite upsetting sometimes because they wouldn't make those assumptions if the two of us being not married just lived in a house by ourselves. They would just assume we were a couple. Whereas I know, like [Geoff

and Trudy], who live in a house by themselves are not a couple. He's
her lodger. [. . .] That is one of the problems which is caused by
living in a collective style. If you care about that sort of thing. I didn't
think I did but increasingly it gets on my nerves.

(Laura [23])

Although several factors contribute to this, other members of the collective
identify the fact that Laura and Chris have separate bedrooms as crucial to
the confusion.

Within the couple, separate bedrooms could have symbolic importance
even if they usually slept together. Both Laura and Chris [23], and Lynne and
Dave [21] mentioned separate bedrooms and the ability to sleep alone or stay
up late reading or whatever. Beth, who also lived in the urban collective, was
considering moving to live with her boyfriend. She would still like her own
space and felt that living in a communal house would be less 'stifling'.

Two women in long-term couple relationships took this further by not
living together and maintaining control over their own space. Allison [28]
reported feeling 'some pressure to live together, not because of other people
so much, but because living apart seemed odd, not quite the normal thing.'
Lisa [26] and her partner are considering buying a joint property but she
states that it must be large enough to have their own space. She also stresses
the importance of not moving into one of the properties they now own
separately. A new property would be neutral.

Several of the women who do not live with men also stress the
importance of their own space. Jane [4] even wonders why she ever thought
she could live with a child, though it has worked out well and Dorothy
respected her space from a very young age. Pat [24] and Miriam [20] are both
divorced. Although Pat sometimes has friends to stay while they are looking
for a place, she does not want to share on a permanent basis. Miriam had a
bad experience with a commune after her divorce and, although she likes the
shared responsibility and companionship of co-owning her house with a
friend, she feels that it is only possible between two (or maybe three) people.
Otherwise it is hard to maintain autonomy. Miriam draws a distinction
between the relationship between co-owners and that with the lodgers.

Two women (Ann [3] and Miriam [20]) now stress the importance of
their living arrangements being women only. Maggie [2] states (less
strongly) that her lodgers are always women. Miriam had had a couple of
short-term male lodgers. Problems with one of them reinforced the earlier
decision that lodgers should be women.

It [having men living in the house] made it a less equal household as far as both of us were concerned. And you're bringing all kinds of power struggles in that I can really do without in the home. I'm quite prepared to battle them out in other places but I want a home to be a nice, safe, comfortable, easy sort of place. I'd really rather keep that out on a permanent basis.

(Miriam)

Ann had lived in several types of living arrangement and now felt it was important to 'work things out with women'. This had influenced her sexuality and she told me she had 'gradually become a lesbian over the last 10 years'.

Ann's life course had included living communally in the 1970s, marrying and realizing the difficulties of 'doing it differently', living communally with children (who were born when she was in a non-cohabiting long-term heterosexual relationship, though they were always *her* children), living on her own, and sharing with one other woman and her children (though not a partner). This sort of change was not uncommon and many of the participants also spoke of several different living arrangements or of a past, conventional relationship as a contrast with the present, anti-sexist one.

Two women (Louise [8] and Lisa [26]) could be said to campaign around the issue of marital status. Louise is a nurse and, in a former job, she and a friend would speak to colleagues about to marry about the option of keeping their own names. Louise recognizes that many of these women still took their husband's names but felt that it was important for them to know they had a choice. Similarly Lisa, in her work as an English teacher in a girls' school, tries to provide images of a variety of living arrangements in the material she uses so that the girls have an opportunity to consider choices. She is appalled by colleagues (especially those who are not married themselves) who just *assume* that the girls will get married.

Marital Status and Women's Liberation

Of the women in the study eight were neither married nor living with a man. 'Single' is perhaps not the best word to describe them as some of them were in long-term (heterosexual) relationships. However, they had all decided not only that they would not marry, but also that they would not live with their partners. In addition, one of the women in the urban collective (Beth) and two of the women in the rural collective (Sara and Eleanor) were single although there were men in their collectives and Beth had a boyfriend.

Tuula Gordon's study reveals that single women value their independence and, even when interested in a couple relationship in principle, refuse the compromises that are involved particularly in heterosexual couple relationships. This is further supported by my evidence. In order to resist being constructed as subordinate to men, women maintain a certain amount of physical, social and emotional space outside of heterosexual couple relationships. This is not easy. Marriage has been seen increasingly as a companionate as well as a domestic and sexual relationship. Miriam [20] had had problems with the co-ownership arrangements when first her friend and then her sister moved out to live with their boyfriends. She acknowledged the strength of the ideal of the couple relationship when she said, 'If you haven't done it, you're obviously going to want to do it'.

Indeed it is this image of marriage which some couples (e.g. Paula and Rob [17]) were trying to live out. That it is an image and not a reality was something that they discovered by encountering resistance and difficulties. For others who married, resistance to marriage often took the form of the woman keeping her own name. Emily Laurence Baker notes that:

> ... the tradition of taking a man's name is the starkest remaining symbol of female inferiority .... a custom originally created to register them as their husband's property.
>
> (1993, p. 13)

Although it is difficult to measure the extent of this practice, it seems to be becoming more common and is often popularly associated with women's rising professional status (Baker, 1993, p. 13).[3] In my study there was systematic variation. Those in role reversals were most likely to be married and to have taken the man's name. In contrast although all but one of the voluntarily childless heterosexual couples were married, none of the women had taken her husband's name. In addition, two of the couples do not tell people that they are married. The heterosexual couples with shared roles are more diverse in this respect with one cohabiting couple, one couple where the woman has taken her husband's name, and two where she has kept her own name. Carolyn and Roger [15] have gone further and given the children her name. This was surprisingly difficult emotionally (for Roger) and illustrates the way that social practices are deeply embedded in our identities.

In much recent sociological research on changing family forms, it is argued that cohabitation is much like marriage. Indeed the standard official statistical classification of family units does not distinguish between married and cohabiting couples. The rise in out-of-wedlock births is said not to be a cause for alarm as many of these are registered to both partners often living at the same address.[4] However, there have been few attempts to verify the similarity between cohabitation and marriage empirically. Certainly to political and moral conservatives, they are not the same thing. Cohabitation lacks the formal, public commitment to a long-term responsibility. Roseanne and John's [5] identification of not being married (and not being 'life-long') as an 'alternative' aspect of their relationship indicates that progressives may also distinguish between them.

Jacqueline Burgoyne (1991) undertook a small study of cohabiting couples. In an article entitled 'Does the ring make any difference?' she notes that while the majority of those who took part in the study considered cohabitation as 'just like a marriage' or even a prelude to marriage, there was a smaller group who did not. This group tended to have more economic advantages than others in her study and:

> ... were more likely to describe themselves and their relationships in studiedly unconventional terms and shared, as a result, a greater preoccupation with the maintenance and development of their identities as individuals.
>
> (Burgoyne, 1991, p. 251)

But the difference between cohabitation and marriage was also notable in her observation that:

> ... those women who did not have access to permanent jobs and who relied, wholly or partially, on being supported economically by their partner, ... [had a] desire, and in some cases considerable anxiety to be legally married.
>
> (1991, p. 253)

One can see that for those women who resist such financial dependence, cohabitation may be preferable. This aspect of marriage will be discussed further in Chapter 6.

Indeed for many the liberatory potential of marriage, or the decision not to marry or not to live with a man, was often related to the more material aspects of the marital relationship. Thus in the rest of the book, the division of housework, the importance and organization of mothering, the orientation to non-domestic work and the distribution of money are explored as practices through which women refuse to be wives. Whether married or not.

Notes

1   The term 'lesbian' only came into use at the end of the period usually referred to as the 'first wave'. Late twentieth-century lesbians have in common with early twentieth-century spinsters their rejection of primary/sexual relations with men and the importance of close relationships with other women (at least).

2   When quoting from interviews I have used the following conventions: '...' indicates discontinuity in the participants' speech; '[...]' indicates that I have omitted part of what they said; anything in square brackets is added by me for clarification; I have put pseudonyms in square brackets in direct quotations.

3   In her article Baker notes that some women who keep their name for professional reasons use their husband's name in their personal lives.

4   In 1989, 71 per cent of births outside marriage were jointly registered of which 72 per cent were to couples giving the same address (Cooper, 1991, p. 14).

Chapter 3

Housework

The principal question to be explored in this chapter is how people divide the housework that they consider needs to be done. This 'nuts and bolts' discussion will be preceded by an examination of how the nature of some tasks can influence the overall division. Issues of knowledge, efficiency, and standards help to explain the arrangements revealed by the empirical findings and will be discussed concurrently. Although one is accustomed to thinking of the division of housework as taking place between one man and one woman, the inclusion of living arrangements with more than two adults introduces more complexity. It became obvious to me that, even in living arrangements which contain only two adults, children are very often included in the division of housework. A specific subsection includes a discussion of the contributions of children and the variations in how much housework children are required to do. The issue of knowledge is particularly important to this discussion. Diane Richardson (1993) has noted that providing role models is a common aspect of anti-sexist child-rearing. Although this topic will be discussed in more detail in Chapter 4, I will consider here the effect of the presence of children, and the images parents wish to give them, on the overall division of housework.

Housework in Feminist and Sociological Research

As I pointed out in Chapter 1, housework was an important focus of early feminist activism and writing and Ann Oakley took the innovative step of studying housework as work. Like sociological studies of other occupations, her focus was on work satisfaction and the way that women organized the routines of their daily occupation. In addition to confirming the dissatisfaction with housework being voiced in the Women's Liberation Movement, her analysis separated feelings about house*work* (predominantly negative) from orientation to the house*wife* role (predominantly medium to highly positive). She also separated housework from mothering and highlighted the incompatibility of the two, a potential challenge to the argument that women's responsibility for the former arose from their biological suitability for (aspects of) the latter (Oakley, 1974a).

The involvement of many British feminists in left-wing politics soon led to attempts to theorize housework within a Marxist framework. Maxine Molyneux (1979) identifies two orientations within this work: 'to show how the subordination of women, ... although often seen as "extra-economic", [is] in fact founded on a *material* basis and is linked into the political economy of capitalist society' (1979, p. 3); and 'identifying the actual and potential role of women within socialist struggle' (1979, p. 4). Owing to the lack of a specific analysis of gender within the work of Marx, feminists had to develop their own analyses. The Domestic Labour Debate, as it became known, contained several strands.

Some discussed whether housework could be conceptualized as productive labour (comparable to waged work, the product being labour power) necessary to capitalism, an oppressor (capitalism) was located and the relationship was theorized. This strand of the debate focused on the value of labour power, its relation to the (male) wage, and the link to the capitalist economic system. The Wages for Housework campaign demanded that it should be paid though the demand has been criticized as simplistic: the sexual division of labour remained unquestioned; the marriage contract and the wage contract were not comparable; and it was unclear *who* would pay these wages (see Kaluzynska, 1980, p. 39).

Materialist feminists (e.g. Delphy, 1977) took the approach of using Marx's methods but theorizing housework as a separate mode of production having its own relations of production. Thus women (as housewives) were oppressed by patriarchy. The maintenance of housewives did not constitute a wage and the unpaid nature of housework was central. This perspective challenged the link between women's oppression and struggle against it, and the oppression and struggle of the proletariat; an analysis which is still being pursued (Delphy and Leonard, 1992; Jackson, 1992).

Other Marxist feminists turned to a re-evaluation of Marx's work on labour process. Women's labour market position as cheap, unskilled workers and/or a reserve army of labour was explained in relation to their position in the home; an advance on Marx's naturalistic explanation based on natural differences of strength and skill. However, this explanation failed to recognize that causality could work in either direction — women's position in the home might be a result of their weak labour market position (Beechey,

1987, Introduction). In most of this literature the link between the public and private spheres was inadequately theorized, resting on a functionalist account which saw women's labour market position as a product of their position in the family.

The Domestic Labour Debate was, in many ways, more about politics than theory. Did unwaged women have a place in the class struggle? Or did women need an autonomous struggle to end their oppression? It was abandoned (though not resolved) and, as Kaluzynska (1980) points out, had become distanced from women anyway. Despite the inability to theorize how housework fits into the capitalist economy, this debate had one positive result: housework is now widely accepted as 'work' both within sociology and within political discourse. In fact the UN has committed itself (on paper at least) to working out how to incorporate it into GNP and other macro-economic indicators although little progress has been made in achieving this goal.[1]

Not all feminist activists had the Marxists' obsession for getting the theory right first. There are two pragmatic 'solutions' to the 'problem' of housework. The first is to reduce the overall amount done and technology is a key element. However, studies have shown that historically this has not had much impact. Rising standards have mitigated the potential liberatory effect of technological innovation in the home (e.g. Cowan, 1989; Thomas and Zmrozcek, 1985).[2]

The other pragmatic solution is to share the work. Some sociological studies of housework take this as their starting point and try to measure both the inequality of the division of housework and changes in that inequality particularly in the light of changing patterns of (married) women's employment (e.g. Gershuny *et al.*, 1986; Kiernan, 1992; Young and Wilmott, 1973). If the Parsonian assumption was of a specialized division of labour between the public and private spheres then what happened when women went out to work or when men lost their jobs? Research interest in dual-earner and dual-career couples usually includes some investigation of the division of housework, and studies of working mothers consider at least the division of those tasks associated with child-care (e.g. Brannen and Moss, 1988, 1991). Indeed the focus of Arlie Hochschild's (1989) study of 'two-job families' is on who does the 'second shift'.

These studies show that even when women are in the paid labour force, they still do the majority of the housework and child-care or are responsible for ensuring that it gets done (e.g. Brannen and Moss, 1991; Hochschild, 1989). Although some studies show that the proportion of domestic work done by husbands of employed women is greater than that done by husbands of non-employed women, others have suggested that this may be due to the reduction in the total amount of housework (Pleck, 1985). Sarah Berk examined a subsample of men who did considerably more housework than other men in her study (and at least as much as the mean amount done by women). Even in these households 'the *relative* position of the wives and husbands ... remained similar to that of the larger sample' (1985, pp. 209–10). It has also been found that unemployed men do less housework than employed men (Morris, 1985; R. Pahl, 1984). The detail of the division has also been fleshed out: men tend to do tasks with clearly defined boundaries, higher leisure components and flexible schedules. They also do those that stay done longer. In addition, men are seen (and see themselves) as 'helping' their wives who have overall responsibility.

While most studies have focused on heterosexual couples (with or without children) and overlook the contribution of children, there have been a few attempts to broaden the understanding to other types of living arrangements. Some American studies have included heterosexual, gay and lesbian couples (e.g. Blumstein and Schwarz, 1983). There have also been studies (usually small) of the division of housework in lesbian and/or gay couples (Coleman and Walters, 1989; Sang, 1984). Studies of communes make only passing reference to the division of labour (see Abrams and McCulloch, 1976).

In general, research into housework focuses on who does which tasks and/or how much time is spent doing them (often in relation to non-domestic work time and leisure time). Explanations are often sought in macro-sociological factors such as class and wife's employment status (e.g. Coverman, 1985; Wright *et al.*, 1992) and very little has been written about the *negotiation* of the division of labour and changes over time.[3] Implicitly or explicitly, a gendered division (on the Parsonian model) acts as the base line. Studies such as those of Hochschild, and Brannen and Moss go further by providing insights into the emotional and ideological processes associated with the division of labour and women's strategies to lessen their burden. However, the preponderance in these studies of women who accept the sexual division of labour in principle limits the scope of the findings.

In feminist terms, what is now required is an analysis which helps to determine *how* women might free themselves from the position Oakley and others documented 20 years ago. This is particularly important in the context of the findings of the British Social Attitudes Survey that, despite a significant rise in the number of people who say that housework *should* be shared, the number who say they *do* share has remained relatively stable (Kiernan, 1992, pp. 105–6).

Most of the recent writing on housework has been empirical. Since the demise of the Domestic Labour Debate little attempt has been made to theorize the continued responsibility of women for housework although several fruitful directions have been indicated. I have found that the materialist feminist analysis provides renewed possibilities especially when linked to other theoretical work (see Chapter 1). Delphy and Leonard theorize housework as the appropriation of women's unpaid labour by the head of household. The 'unpaid' quality derives not from the particular tasks involved but from the social relations within which those tasks are done (Delphy and Leonard, 1992, p. 95). Women's position within those social relations is in the role of wife. It must be emphasized that the labour involved is not necessarily appropriated by the person for whom the labour is done but, rather, by the head of household. This formulation allows us to distinguish self-caring from servicing and the immediate recipient of work from the appropriator of the labour – which is particularly important if we are to imagine caring for those who cannot care for themselves (e.g. the very young, the very ill) in non-oppressive ways. Strategically, one can begin to imagine the possibility of the same tasks, which are often necessary for the maintenance of daily life or a particular standard of living, being done within different social relations.

The people in my study are resisting and rejecting the role/identity of wife and its complement, the head of household. This effort has included changing the division of housework in various ways. In this chapter, I will consider the anti-sexist character of these new divisions of housework, what they tell us about the social relations which they are rejecting, and how far such change is possible.

Analytical Categories

In addition to the categories of types of living arrangement which I will use throughout this study, I have found it necessary to create a second set of analytical categories for the treatment of housework. My categories differ significantly from some of those used in research on housework. For example, Gregson and Lowe (1993) use a typology based on the frequency and importance of tasks. My categories emerged from the interview material and reflected the way tasks were grouped by participants in discussion. Like Marjorie DeVault (1990), I have tried to think in terms that make sense to the people doing the housework. I have divided housework into three types: child-care, activities related to eating, and cleaning. 'Activities related to eating' include cooking, shopping, setting and clearing the table, and washing up. The category 'cleaning' includes laundry and cleaning the house (dusting, vacuuming, etc.) but not washing up. Other activities such as maintenance and decorating were mentioned rarely in the interviews. For purposes of analysis they will be considered within the cleaning category.

Gardening forms a significant part of the division of housework for three living arrangements. In two of these it is considered with activities related to eating because of the nature of the garden, in the third it is considered as 'other'.

In interviews I asked very general questions about how housework was divided and how much housework was done. Thus I only have information on tasks participants thought were important. I have taken into account the things people said they did not do as well as what they did do. Existing studies of working mothers have noted the strategy of reducing the total amount of housework (Brannen and Moss, 1991; Hochschild, 1989). This reduction may be accomplished either by lowering standards or by employing someone else to do some of the work. Most living arrangements achieved comparable standards although Christiane and Wilhelm [11],[4] a role reversal, kept their house immaculate (it was hard to believe that two children under five lived there) and Carol and Patrick [14], also a role reversal, did much more ironing than anyone else. The amount of housework actually done by the members of the living arrangements, however, varies owing to the employment of paid cleaners by some.

Overview by Type of Arrangement

The anti-sexist nature of single mother living arrangements is not immediately apparent from the material considered here. However, if we think of the sexist nature of the division of housework in terms of the servicing of adults and children for the head of household, their situation may be construed as the taking of individual responsibility for housework. Child-care, in particular, and the contributions of children to housework were the primary considerations for these women. The four women had very different arrangements but the availability of support from friends or relatives who are not living with them was important to all.

For the voluntarily childless heterosexual couples child-care is obviously not an issue. In this category we can see both the distinction between cleaning and activities related to eating, and the different methods of dividing housework. The division of housework amongst heterosexual couples with children with shared roles is similar to that of the voluntarily childless couples with the addition of child-care.

Amongst the heterosexual couples with children in role reversal situations, there is an implicit belief that a division between paid work and domestic work is not *per se* oppressive to women but that the gendered assumptions surrounding that division are. Child-care is often the primary consideration and influences the division of other types of housework and non-domestic work. In all of the living arrangements in this category one parent does much more child-care than the other. Most of the other housework is done by the same person.

Where there are more than two adults it is more difficult to fall into stereotyped patterns although gender socialization may still affect the division of housework. Differences within this group are related to the origin of the arrangements. Two are modifications of a nuclear family household and are perhaps more likely to have a stronger influence from traditional understandings. The others have differing commitments to gender equality and different relationships between the various members of the living arrangement which affect the division of housework. For most of the 'other' living arrangements the division of housework is similar to that for single mothers by choice — individual responsibility.

The Nature of the Work

Different types of housework enter into the calculation of an equal or fair division of housework with different statuses. Child-care is similar to cleaning, cooking and fixing the car in that there is work to be done which takes time and effort. Some of that work is at least as menial and unpleasant as other housework (e.g. washing nappies). However, 'child-care' can also be 'time spent with the children' and valued for the relationship. Enjoyment is also an important consideration for activities related to eating, especially cooking. Although cleaning has little or no emotional content for those in my study, the nature of some tasks does influence who takes responsibility for them.

The influence of the nature of child-care on the division of all housework is marked for heterosexual couples with children in role reversals. The desire of the women in this group to spend time with their children leads to a division of labour that, were the genders reversed, we would see as contributing to the oppression of women as housewives. For example, Rebecca [12] notes the importance of spending time with her daughter in the evenings and at weekends because her role as primary earner keeps her out of the house through the week. She feels that this is more important than doing the cleaning so Jack does almost all of the other housework although she tends to help out when she is on holiday. In their calculations, child-care is treated as an important relationship for which time must be found for both of them. The potential contradictions of this division are illustrated by a lesbian couple, Amy and Kathryn [28]. They are constantly evaluating and adjusting their division of housework because, although they feel strongly that the one who has been out at work all week should have the weekend to spend time with the children, they are aware of feminist arguments about housework and are also trying to avoid a situation where one person is servicing the other one and the children.

Because the division of child-care for heterosexual couples with shared roles was more equal, it does not have implications for the division of other tasks. In the one situation (Alice and Roy [16]) where one person is currently spending more time during the week with the children, Alice finds the time at the weekends by giving up other *non-domestic* activities.

The enjoyment (or not) of cooking clearly influenced the division of activities related to eating. For those who couldn't cook and didn't enjoy it, cooking was rare or confined to convenience foods (e.g. Roseanne and John [5], Kate [1]). Similarly where all enjoy cooking, the task is likely to be shared either by cooking together or alternating regularly (e.g. Paula and Rob [17], Carol and Patrick [14]). In contrast, because Peg [7] enjoys cooking, she and Ian swap tasks related to eating.

There is some evidence of the constructed nature of enjoyment. Prior to the evolution of their current arrangements, Val did all of the cooking in the Peterson household [22] and remarked that she has *only recently realized* that she herself does *not* like cooking although she is a good cook. In addition, it was clear that enjoyment may be encouraged after the fact. Jason and Margaret make an excursion of the shopping perhaps going out for lunch as well; Jason says he enjoys shopping. Laura's situation in the urban collective [19] also highlights the effects of context. She thinks that her enjoyment of cooking (and consequent larger share) is related to working from home which feels temporary (although it is not).

The division of cleaning was more likely to be influenced by issues of knowledge, standards and efficiency (discussed below) than enjoyment. However, for the most part, in those living arrangements where one or more people are home most of the time it is that person who is responsible for general tidying.[5] Although some relate this to standards (e.g. Jack [12]), it can also be explained by the ill-defined nature of the task. Tidying is not a discrete task and is more likely to be done intermittently while doing other things. The tendency for responsibility to fall to the person(s) at home all day may be taken into account in the overall division (e.g. Karen and Pete [6]) or not (e.g. the urban collective [19]). The invisibility of the task is evident in the latter situation.

It seems that the pleasurable nature of some activities can influence the entire division of labour. In particular, the dual nature of child-care as both work and relationship can lead to an unequal division of other housework in order to equalize the time spent with the children. This is particularly obvious in role reversals. The other task which seems to be assigned at least partly based on enjoyment is cooking. As we shall see later, this poses an interesting question about how it is valued in an exchange. Val's [22] comment about cooking alerts us to the constructed nature of that enjoyment.

These findings contrast sharply with other studies. It is usually found that if there is a 'nice' and 'nasty' division, or a difference in prestige, the nicer and higher prestige tasks are usually taken by the man leaving the rest (usually the bulk of the housework) to the woman. In my study it appears that cooking is divided based on enjoyment when all the adults in a living arrangement do not agree on whether or not it is 'nice' and thus if one person thinks it is, they get to do it. Indeed enjoyment of cooking varies widely within the study and where all the adults dislike it, much less cooking gets done either through the use of convenience foods or eating out.

Most surprising are the findings regarding the influence of child-care on other housework. True role reversals are rarely found in sociological studies. The discovery of men in 'Parsonian' style families who spent a lot of their spare time with their children has been treated as exceptional (e.g. Young and Wilmott, 1973). Most studies have found that even if men do child-care while their wives do non-domestic work, the women remain responsible for the other housework (e.g. Russell, 1987). The child-care men do may also be limited to the 'nicer' aspects. Similarly, in studies of dual-earner households, men may make an effort to spend a lot of time with children but the rest of the housework is rarely divided (Brannen and Moss, 1991; Hochschild, 1989). I have not come across any studies in which making time for someone to spend time with the children was cited as a reason for doing the bulk of the housework. With this in mind, I now turn to the detail of the arrangements.

Ways of Dividing Housework

Even within traditional households there are some tasks which would be seen as individual responsibilities unless someone was physically incapable of performing them (e.g. brushing teeth, going to the toilet). It was evident that amongst the participants in my study the number of tasks for which members of the living arrangement were individually responsible was expanded. The low level of individual responsibility in conventional living arrangements is illustrated by this quote from one of the participants in Sarah Berk's study:

> Never. He never helps me. I suppose I should say 'rarely.' That's a better word to describe it. He hangs up his clothes once in a while. He puts his dirty socks down the laundry chute. In extreme

circumstances, he makes the bed. He does nothing. He doesn't have to. It's not his job.

(1985, p. 205)

Expanding its scope to include the activities mentioned here and others like them has enormous potential. The strategy of increasing the scope of individual responsibility is limited, however, by the communal nature of some space and the desire of some to eat as a group.

For those tasks which could not be individually attributed, there were two methods of division. Sharing involves all adults doing all types of work; swapping involves each individual having responsibility for specific tasks. In a given living arrangement different methods may be used for different types of housework. The division of cleaning and child-care may be with adults internal and external to the residential group, both paid and unpaid. Sharing may sometimes appear to be swapping (for example cooking for washing up) but with the tasks alternating regularly.[6] In contrast, what I call swapping would be characterized by one person taking constant responsibility for certain tasks. It is in the category of cleaning and other housework that the modes of swapping and sharing become most obvious. In interviews the difference is often apparent: those who swap can more readily list specific tasks and assign them to an individual; those who share are more likely to say things like 'We clean the house together on Sundays'.

Someone must decide how much housework needs to be done. The issue of standards may be affected by the physical location of different members of a living arrangement. Do your standards change if you are home all day? It may also be an effect of personal history (socialization) and may be heavily gendered. When deciding how that work will be divided the abilities of individuals may be taken into consideration. Does someone take responsibility for a particular task because they are the only one who knows how to do it? Or because they do it better and more efficiently? This issue is often treated differently for adults than for children. What follows is an analysis of the various solutions arrived at according to living arrangement. The contributions of children are considered separately in a later section.

Single Mothers by Choice

Because there is only one adult in these living arrangements, any division of housework is either with people outside the residential group or between the single mother and the children. In the case of child-care the primary factor is whether it is taken on solely by the single parent or whether other adults have some input. The details are shown in Table 3.1. For most of the women in this category out of school child-care is shared either with a paid child-minder, or with friends and/or relatives. The primary responsibility seems to lie with the mother and she is responsible for the division of labour in this area.

Activities related to eating are rarely discussed in this category. Most cooking falls to the adult although Ann's children [3] can get simple meals when necessary (for example, when she was ill). Kate's arrangement [1] is the only one where activities related to eating are considered an individual responsibility. They live mostly on convenience foods and never eat a meal together. Maggie's daughter [2] clears the table and Ann's children do the washing up.

The main issue for single mothers by choice concerning cleaning is whether or not children should do any (discussed below). Maggie [2] hires someone half a day per week to do the major cleaning. Standards affect the amount of housework done. None of them does a lot of cleaning.

Voluntarily Childless Heterosexual Couples

In Table 3.2 we see a complex mix of swapping and sharing of activities related to eating, though with some unequal swaps, and a slight tendency for

Table 3.1: Division of child-care in single mother living arrangements

	Participant	Internal	External	
			Paid	Unpaid
1	Kate — 1st daughter	A friend lived with her for a year	Tried but didn't work out	Mother, sister
	2nd daughter	Older daughter (a.m. and paid babysitting)	Nursery	Occasional
2	Maggie	Lodgers occasionally	Full-time child-minder (now afterschool care)	Support of mother, sisters and aunt
3	Ann — early	Collective child-care in commune	None	None
	— now	(Recently started to share flat)	Child-minder (no more than 2 hours/week)	Children's father some weekends and one-week holiday
4	Jane	None	None	Nursery (free owing to daughter's disability); mother (rarely)

Housework

women to cook more. There is considerable variety in the strategies used to divide these tasks: two couples swap, two share and one takes individual responsibility.

I have already discussed the influence of enjoyment in this area. Knowledge and efficiency are also commonly raised in relation to activities related to eating. Neither Roseanne nor John [5] is a good cook and both have 'limited repertoires'. This lies behind the frequent use of convenience foods and restaurants and the division of what little cooking they do based on the ability to cook a particular meal. Similarly, Peg's [7] responsibility for cooking is explained by her ability (in addition to enjoyment). It also effects the amount of work involved; they eat quite elaborate meals. In contrast with the findings of most studies (e.g. Morris, 1985; Pahl, 1984), Ian took over this task when he was unemployed.

In Table 3.3. we see that cleaning is primarily swapped although paid help is also used. When cleaning is shared it is often done by alternating who does particular tasks.

In this category only Peg [7] raises the issue of who organizes the dividing. Although her responsibility for organizing the division of labour sometimes bothers her, she explains it with reference to her higher standards. Louise's [8] higher standards ('fastidiousness') are an important determinant of their unequal division of housework. Karen and Pete [6] have an interesting reversal of this situation. Karen doesn't do any of Pete's ironing partly because he doesn't think her ironing is up to his standards.[7] She also says that she can't see dust so vacuuming and dusting fall to Pete. Louise and Mark's division also illustrates the failure of technology as a solution to

Table 3.2: Division of activities related to eating in voluntarily childless heterosexual couples

	Cooking		Washing-up	Shopping	Swap or share
	Week	Weekend			
5	Convenience foods; eating out	Alternates with washing-up	Alternates with cooking	Together	Share
6	Individual responsibility	Shared; eat out	Unknown	Unknown	Indiv. resp.
7	Peg	Peg	Ian	Ian	Swap
8	Louise (Mark makes lunch sandwiches)		Both	Louise	Swap?
9	Alternates with washing-up; Barbara takes lunch and afternoon tea in college		Alternates with cooking (or whoever gets fed up first)	Unknown	Share

Table 3.3: The division of cleaning in voluntarily childless heterosexual couples

	Swap		Share	Indiv. resp.	Paid
	Man	Woman			
5	Washing to the laundry	Houseplants	None	Ironing	Yes
6	Vacuuming, dusting, repair jobs	Washing, tidying, waits in for contractors	None	Ironing	No
7	Unclear — split what cleaner doesn't do; Peg organizes			Ironing	Yes
8		Most (mentions vacuuming, washing)	None	Unknown	No[1]
9			Cleaning (Juan more)	Washing, ironing	No[2]

[1] They have the paper delivered.
[2] There is a cleaner but she doesn't come often so I have treated them as if they do not employ anyone.

women's responsibility for housework. The purchase of a 'labour saving device' added another task to Louise's list of responsibilities: before they had a washing machine Mark did the washing by hand.

Karen and Pete [6] are the only ones in this category to mention physical location as influential, perhaps because most people work outside the home. The tasks for which Karen is responsible are those which are compatible with her work pattern. Karen explains Pete's responsibility for repair jobs as related to her lack of knowledge. It is interesting that Pete mumbled that he didn't know what he was doing either and that Karen refers to these as 'manly things' indicating that there is an expectation of knowledge which is gendered.

Activities related to both eating and cleaning may be reduced by various means. Many people in this group do not cook regularly. The difference in preparation time of convenience foods also reduces the amount of labour divided. For most these activities seem to be shared although in two couples the woman is responsible for cooking with the man taking some or all the responsibility for other related activities. Cleaning can be reduced by employing someone. Also some activities in this area seem to be considered individual responsibilities (notably laundry and ironing). Sharing of cleaning activities is not common in this group although little mention is made of the logic behind the swapping of the tasks. Only Peg [7] mentions that it should be 'fair'.

Heterosexual Couples with Children in Role Reversal Situations

There was a strong desire by couples in this category to look after the children themselves. The division of child-care is thus usually between the two partners. However, most of the couples also use some outside child-care. Playgroup-type child-care was mentioned by Liz and Steve [10], and Rebecca and Jack [12]. Liz and Steve's eldest child went to a child-minder one day a week; Christiane and Wilhelm [11] have an au pair/mother's help. The men do most of the child-care internal to the residential group although the women often take over at weekends and in the evenings. They are quite explicit about compensating both for the time they spend away from their children and for the time their partners spend doing child-care. Carol [14] is a strong example of the latter motivation; Rebecca [12], the former.

Child-care is the only activity in which an effort is made to involve both partners more equally. As noted earlier, this has an impact on the division of other housework. Very little explanation of the division of labour, which resembles a traditional division in many ways, is given. The only time explanations are given is when the woman takes on some housework which would otherwise be assumed to fall to the man. Liz and Steve [10] say that it is just as reasonable for her to go out to work and him to take care of the children and the house as the reverse would be. This contrasts with studies which confirm how widespread the belief is that men are unable to take on 'women's role' in the home (e.g. Brannen and Moss, 1988, 1991).

In this category the most common division of activities related to eating is the swap. In most cases this is almost a misnomer unless one considers housework to have been swapped for paid work as in most of these living arrangements the man has almost complete responsibility for domestic tasks.

Liz and Steve [10] are the only ones in this category who don't eat together. Liz cooks her own meals, usually convenience foods. Steve makes the children's food. Sunday dinner is an exception and either one might prepare it. The amount of work involved for Christiane and Wilhelm [11] is much reduced by the au pair/mother's help who cooks the children's main meal at midday reducing their responsibility to deciding what it will be. Wilhelm does breakfast, a cold meal in the evening, and the washing up. Christiane sweeps up around the table after every meal, because of her standards. The exceptional task in Carol and Patrick's [14] arrangements is shopping now that Carol drives to work. She also usually cooks at weekends.

The men in role reversals also do the lion's share of the cleaning. Only Christiane and Wilhelm [11] have paid help. They also have the highest standards. The others describe themselves as 'scruffy side of average' (Jack

[12]), 'low priority' (Carol [14]), or 'do it when it needs it' (Steve [10]). Only Patrick [14] does a lot of ironing (including Carol's), a task which in other living arrangements is an individual responsibility and/or rarely done. The women often do 'one-off' cleaning jobs. If being in the house most of the day affects one's standards of cleanliness, we would expect to see some evidence in this group. Only Jack mentions that untidiness bothers him more now that he is home most of the time. 'Exceptional' tasks may be taken on for reasons of knowledge, efficiency and/or standards. For example, Rebecca [12] does the laundry because Jack puts everything in together regardless of instructions on the label and would ruin some of her clothes. Disagreements about these issues can be potentially destructive. Lucy [26] writes of their difference of opinion regarding housework leading to her doing the bulk of it and proclaiming the role reversal 'an exhausting failure'.

Heterosexual Couples with Children with Shared Roles

For the couples with shared roles, the principle that both will do child-care is strongly affected in practice by the nature of their non-domestic work. The lack of flexible non-domestic work influences each partner's availability to do their share.[8] The resulting division is shown in Table 3.4.

Jean and Eric [18] both work freelance from home and can take Mick with them to most of the meetings that they attend. Carolyn [15] has tended to do more child-care owing to her difficulty in finding work and Roger's full-time employment. This situation should change now that their non-domestic work situation has improved. Because Roy [16] is a teacher, it is quite easy for him to be home at the same time as the children most days and to be there in school holidays. Since Alice [16] has been working full time she has followed a pattern similar to the women in role-reversal situations

Table 3.4: *The division of child-care in heterosexual couples with shared roles*

	Internal	External	
		Paid	Unpaid
15	Shared (Carolyn more)	No	School nursery
16	Roy after school; Alice weekends	No	Older friend
17	Share (Rob slightly more)	Nursery, child-minder	No
18	Share; short-term contracts with each other	No	Friend, Jean's mother

and made a commitment to spending weekends doing things with the children.

All of the couples with shared roles share activities related to eating. Both Jean and Eric [18], and Carolyn and Roger [15] alternate cooking. Rob and Paula [17] both cook, often together. Roy [16] cooks weekdays and he and Alice share the cooking at weekends. No one in this group mentions washing up specifically except Jean and Eric [18] who list it as one of the 'essential' cleaning tasks. Paula and Rob [17] shop together but both Roy [16] and Roger [15] do the shopping in their respective living arrangements.

Although all the living arrangements in this category share child-care and activities related to eating, cleaning is shared by some and swapped by others. It also emerges that the division of housework may be more thought out in some living arrangements than in others. Both Jean and Eric [18], and Paula and Rob [17] say that they don't do much cleaning and have no formal way of deciding who does what. Alice and Roy [16] are the only ones to use paid help. They are also the only couple to swap tasks. Roy found it difficult to find his place domestically in a settled home[9] but it was important to do his share because of his commitment to feminist politics. Alice manages the division, does the washing, mending and a lot of the less tangible things. Roy is responsible for any cleaning not done by the paid cleaner, and the ironing.

In this category there is a more general questioning of differences in standards, knowledge and efficiency. Carolyn [15] points out that it might be possible to swap tasks at some point in the future but is critical of the reasons why one might be better at some things or enjoy some things more than others. They insist on getting back to a base of equality. They also emphasize the evolution of Roger taking on responsibility and thinking about what needs to be done as well as doing it. For example, in the past Carolyn had to remind Roger to think about when the laundry might need to be done, but now he thinks of this (and does it) himself.

In contrast Paula and Rob [17] see equality as a given rather than something to be fought for. They talk about their relationship as a partnership and their division of labour as obvious: they both do everything; they take turns informally; it just works out. They do mention experience as affecting the division of child-care tasks. Rob had younger siblings and was more comfortable with the care of children than Paula who had had no contact with children before Jeremy was born. They also note that cooking was something that they learned to do together and enjoy doing together.

There are still some conflicts. Roy [16] notes that although he and Alice broadly agree about standards, areas like the bathroom are contentious. Carolyn and Roger [15] disagree over whether the children's clothes need to be ironed. Roger doesn't think that ironing is necessary so Carolyn irons all the children's clothes. There are also conflicts based on knowledge and efficiency. Alice [16] does mending because Roy doesn't know how and she is quicker at it. Similarly, Roger [15] has never learned to sew so if it is to be done Carolyn has to do it.

Women deal with the gendered nature of knowledge, efficiency and standards in different ways. Carolyn [15] notes how she no longer thinks that Roger gets the wrong things when he goes shopping. She obviously fought these feelings until she accepted his abilities. However, Alice [16] finds it easier to hire a cleaner than to have Roy do the cleaning.

Sharing is the dominant strategy in this category although the motivations may be very different. For some (e.g. Carolyn and Roger [15]) it is to overcome differences in standards and abilities; for others (e.g. Paula and Rob [17]) it is a reflection of their equality. Although not as obvious as in the role reversals, child-care does affect this situation as a desire to share child-care equally influences their preferred non-domestic work arrangements and the sharing of other domestic work.

Multiple Adult Arrangements

The diversity within this category is reflected in the division of housework. In addition, the Peterson household [22] has only evolved in an anti-sexist way since child-care has been reduced. The division of child-care, shown in Table 3.5, seems to be unchanged by the existence of other adult members of a living arrangement except that they are available informally. When both parents live in the arrangement the division will be similar to couples in other sorts of arrangements; otherwise, the mother has primary responsibility.

Amongst the few for whom knowledge and efficiency affect the division of child-care tasks are Lynne and Dave [21]. They tended to swap child-care tasks according to their strengths. When the children were younger Dave was more likely to do outdoor and practical things with them and Lynne was more likely to teach them to sew or read to them, a traditional division. Because Lynne cannot drive, Dave drove them places. Now that the children are older and their needs are primarily emotional, child-care tasks are shared.

Activities related to eating are dependent on the social arrangement of eating and are shown in Table 3.6.

There are disputes about knowledge, efficiency and standards in the Peterson household [22]. However, despite differences there has been no change in the division of housework. When they go shopping Jason and Margaret seem (to Val) to forget things and get a lot of the wrong things because neither is a particularly good cook nor enjoys cooking so they have

Table 3.5: The division of child-care in multiple adult arrangements

	Internal		External	
	Primary	Other	Paid	Unpaid
19	(No children)			
20	Miriam (mother)	Lodgers baby-sit occasionally	Not now	School, neighbour, Becki's father
21	Dave (father)	Lynne (mother) stops work when kids home from school	No	Lodgers
22	Val (mother)	Margaret, Jason (father)	No	No
23	Mary (mother)	All others (various activities and baby-sitting)	No	Mention kids' father and grandparents

Table 3.6: The division of activities related to eating in multiple adult arrangements

	Social arrangement	Cooking	Washing-up	Shopping	Other
19	Indiv. resp. (couples eat together)	Indiv. resp. (Jackie and Julian together; Laura more than Chris)	Dishwasher (last in turns on)	Indiv. resp. (some communal)	
20	Indiv. resp. (Miriam and Becki together)	Indiv. resp. (Miriam for Becki)	Indiv. resp.	Indiv. resp.	Garden: co-owners
21	Non-compulsory communal meal	Dave	Not mentioned	Dave	
22	Non-compulsory communal meal (Sunday together)	Alternate (no fixed rota)	Jason	Jason and Margaret	Margaret works out shopping money
23	Non-compulsory communal meal	Alternate (rota)	Alternate (not cook)	Mostly Mary	Eleanor sets breakfast table; gardening shared (Sara and Alex heavy jobs)

no sense of the staple things that need to be in the cupboards. Similarly, although Jason finds cooking difficult and time-consuming, and it requires him to stop working, this does not prevent him from doing his share.

Jason's responsibility for washing up is partly due to his belief that they should not use the dishwasher.[10] He takes responsibility for doing it by hand.

Val would prefer to have the surfaces and sink free of dishes most of the time, which they are not, but has not taken over the job. Jason does not appear to use knowledge or standards as a 'strategy' to reduce his involvement (cf. Hochschild, 1989, pp. 201–3) and Val doesn't feel that it is her responsibility to ensure that it gets done 'properly'.[11]

The balance between Laura and Chris, in the urban collective [19], is related to Laura's enjoyment of cooking. In the rural collective [23], efficiency affects the amount of washing up that Alex does. Although in principle the cook doesn't wash up, Alex explains that it is easier and quicker for him to do it while he's cooking than for someone else to come in later.

The most common way of dividing cleaning and other activities, shown in Table 3.7, seems to be the swap. Tasks are divided up and assigned to individual members. None of the arrangements in this category had a rota for cleaning in which tasks were routinely changed although some had tried it in the past. Rather than swapping or sharing cleaning tasks, the urban collective [19] rely on the principle of collective responsibility, a sort of cross between individual responsibility and sharing.

> We rely on people's idea of collective responsibility. You can laugh but I think it's true. We're all responsible for each other. The trouble with that breaks down when you have people like [a couple currently living there] who don't have an idea of collective responsibility at all and will only clear up their own mess and become very very annoyed if somebody else hasn't cleared up their own mess and then sort of spitefully don't clear up their mess either and the whole thing escalates. While everyone's doing their own thing and sort of covering each other slightly it holds up.
>
> (Laura)

The impact of being at home more sometimes has an effect. Laura remarks that because she is home all day the mess gets on her nerves and she does a lot of tidying. This annoys her from time to time primarily because it is invisible work. Although she doesn't explain it, Mary [23] mentioned that she had ended up doing most of the cleaning in the rural collective. The fact that she was correcting Alex's report that it was shared by all members of the collective illustrates the invisibility of this work. Val says that she feels differently about housework now that she is working full time. Although previously she felt responsible for it even though she didn't do much, now she doesn't feel responsible at all.

Table 3.7: The division of cleaning in multiple adult arrangements

	Indiv. resp.	Swap	Share	Paid
19	Unknown		Collective resp. for communal space	No
20	Own rooms	Lodgers, hall and kitchen floor; one co-owner, 2 downstairs rooms; other, bathroom and downstairs toilet; responsibility with co-owners	Some tasks (unspecified); maintenance and decorating between co-owners; take things for recycling	No
21	Own rooms	Lynne, washing, ironing, directs children's cleaning; Dave, maintenance		Yes (2/wk)
22	Ironing (Jenny's done by Val)	Margaret and Jason tidy; Jason vacuums, waits in for tradespeople, cats to vet; Margaret houseplants and gardening; Val, cut flowers, washing, piano tuner		No
23	Unknown	Children collect kindling, bring wood in from shed; Sara most chopping (also Alex); Alex a lot of carrying	Cleaning (in principle); collect wood	No

Other Living Arrangements

Because the other women in this category live alone they make little mention of housework. Pat [24] eats mostly take-aways and convenience foods, washes up once a week and cleans in occasional bursts. Both Lisa [25] and Allison [27] are not sharing a household with their partners so each is responsible for their own space.[12] Meals eaten with their partners are cooked by the person whose flat they are eaten in. However, Allison makes an interesting observation about the domestic division of labour.

> I am 5'2" and he is 6'4" — my flat is full of small things, and he has built up all his kitchen surfaces, etc. to be a good working height for him. Its difficult to imagine how we could share a kitchen, just from that point of view. (Maybe that's why women end up in the kitchen?)

Although perhaps never the whole explanation, it indicates the contribution that the construction of our physical space can make to efficiency and thus to the division of housework.

Determinants and Consequences of Different Methods

The division of housework does not appear to be based on a traditional gendered division although there are various methods of reaching an equal division. Delphy and Leonard (1992) have demonstrated that the oppression of housewives is not inherent in the work that they perform but rather is located in the social relations under which they perform them. All of these methods reject the social relations in which the head of household is serviced by his dependents (primarily his wife). By expanding the number of tasks for which members of a living arrangement take individual responsibility, the right of any member to benefit from the services of a wife is resisted. In living arrangements with children this may involve a re-evaluation of the abilities of children. The limits on this strategy are related to the communal aspect of some space and activities and thus it can only apply to all housework in those living arrangements with only one person. It is the primary strategy of single mothers by choice but also forms an important part of all living arrangements.

The swap deals with the problem of communal space and activities by dividing housework between individual members of the household in such a way that each individual has responsibility for a specified set of communal tasks. A standard of equivalence must be introduced in order to evaluate the equality or fairness of this arrangement. Various problems arise in the attempt to do this and these could be seen as evidence of the usual absence of such calculation.[13]

One such problem is that the nature of some tasks renders them invisible. This has already been noted regarding general tidying but is also relevant for less tangible tasks including organizing the division of housework. The urban collective [19] indicate another potential problem: to whom do the irregular tasks (like leaving a note for the milk delivery) fall? The pleasurable nature of some tasks can affect their value. If you enjoy cooking is its value as work reduced? Is the fact that you cook rather elaborate meals taken into account or dismissed as a personal preference?

Differences in abilities can also raise problems. Peg [7] mentions a logic of the time taken to do things as entering into their calculation of a 'fair swap' for cooking. However, if one person takes longer because of their lower ability, is the task more valued? Standards can also affect the allocation of value. If more work is involved because of higher standards what is a 'fair' swap? None of these questions is adequately addressed by those who used this method of dividing the housework.

In contrast with other studies the ability to do child-care does not seem to arise as a determinant of the division except for Paula and Rob [17] and, in a different way, Lynne and Dave [21]. This is perhaps because of its dual nature as a relationship which both parents want to foster. Of the tasks that need to be done regularly only ironing, laundry and cooking arise as tasks taken on because of differences in abilities or standards and then not frequently. They are also the tasks most likely to be an individual responsibility. Other tasks divided on this basis are less regular — mending clothes, repairing the roof, etc.

Sharing avoids some of these problems. The term 'collective responsibility', used by the urban collective [19], seems to capture the logic of this method. As they point out, it is flexible enough to take irregular tasks into account, and the necessity of determining the value of tasks is avoided. Over time all members of a living arrangement will do equal amounts of all tasks. In addition, as Carolyn and Roger emphasize [15], it can be used to overcome differences in abilities and preferences. The problem of standards must be resolved, and Carolyn and Roger's continuing disagreement about ironing illustrates the potential difficulties. The primary drawback to this strategy is that it can mask continuing inequalities.

The most interesting finding is the differential impact of knowledge and efficiency on the division of housework between adults and on the contributions of children. Although some adults make an effort to counter the gendered nature of differences, most have some division of labour based on differences in abilities. However, contributions of children to housework are often seen as important because of their need to acquire skills even in living arrangements which do not question differences of abilities amongst adults. The issue of efficiency is also interesting in this respect as it is more efficient to do tasks oneself than to teach someone else how to do them or resolve differences in standards.

Children and Housework

Although some studies of children have drawn attention to their performance of housework for extra money (O'Brien, forthcoming), very little attention seems to have been paid to their involvement in housework generally, and they are virtually ignored in research on housework. In addition to any contribution they might make, children's presence can influence the division of housework in three ways: (1) by adding to the total amount of work to be done, (2) by the influence of child-care on the division of other tasks, and (3) by the desire to influence children's behaviour in a particular way. I remind the reader that I did not interview children under 18 and, thus, this section relies on the reports of adults.

Children's Contributions

Children's contributions to housework were not always explicitly mentioned though sometimes they were implied. In five living arrangements the children were too young (by anyone's judgment) to do housework. Only one child in my study, Ruth [1], was involved in child-care in her own living arrangement. This is usually because children have no siblings, are too young to take part in child-care activities, or the age difference between children is small. However, children were regularly mentioned in relation to both activities related to eating, and cleaning.

Washing up and setting and/or clearing the table were mentioned or implied as something children of varying ages did. In some cases children were also involved in cooking. Ann [3] and Lynne and Dave [21] mentioned that their children were capable of getting their own meals if necessary but were not regularly expected to cook. The Peterson children (the youngest of whom was 13 and who are perhaps better described as young adults) were included in the informal rota of cooking for the family. Kate's children got their own meals on a regular basis. Both Steve [10] and Roy [16] encouraged the children to help with cooking. Most children older than about six were responsible for cleaning their own rooms though with varying inputs from adults regarding standards and supervision. Many participants also mentioned that the children either did or should do other unspecified cleaning tasks.

Several issues impact on whether and how much housework children do including the need to acquire skills, the work involved in getting children to do things, and the emotional impact on the child. Often these were in conflict with each other. Most parents wanted their children to acquire the skills necessary to run a house. This was thought particularly important for boys and was often related to the recognition of the effect the adults' own upbringing had had on their current division of housework. This motivation was mentioned by Ann [3], Liz [10], and Alice and Roy [16]. However, this was in contradiction both with the work involved in organizing the children to do housework, and the memory of being forced to do 'chores' as a child. Maggie [2], Kate [1], and Steve [10] all mention the former; Alice [16], the latter.

Children rarely make decisions about how much housework needs to be done, or who will do it. The exception is in the case of their own rooms. Children were often responsible for cleaning their own rooms and both Alice and Roy [16], and Lynne and Dave [21] said that they didn't set standards for the children's rooms. However, Ann [3], whose children are younger, sets standards so they will acquire skills.

The kids feel that they've got a right to keep their room a mess. Well, I say that they've only got that right when they've learnt how not to keep it a mess. It's not a positive choice.

(Ann)

This forms part of a wider strategy to increase the amount of housework which is an individual responsibility and relates to the importance of raising children to be independent.[14]

This link is most obvious in Kate's living arrangement [1]. Although Kate is a single mother, activities related to eating are an individual responsibility. Children learn to get their own meals at a relatively young age. Similarly, Lynne and Dave's [21] children are capable of getting their own meals if they are not present for the communal meal, relieving them of the responsibility of ensuring that the children are fed.

The issue of knowledge and efficiency is particularly important. One motivation for getting children to do housework was the perceived need for them to acquire the skills necessary to keep a house. Thus, for children, it was a *lack* of knowledge that led to them being required to do housework. The issue of efficiency arises in opposition to the acquisition of knowledge. Both Steve [10] and Kate [1] found it easier to do the housework themselves than to organize the children to do it.

Children's Influence on the Division of Housework

Children seem to have a contradictory influence on the division of housework in the living arrangements studied. On the one hand they increase the total amount of work to be done, especially when they are very young. As they get older they may be treated as an extra individual to be included in the division of all the work. However, the work involved in teaching children how to do housework and organizing them can also be seen to increase the amount of work involved.

I have already discussed the influence of adults' perception of the importance of spending time with the children on the overall division of labour. However, child-care is not an issue that can be thought of purely in terms of the adults in a living arrangement. Although dishes don't care who washes them, children often care who looks after them. Children can also have views about other housework. Lynne [21] points out that although she hasn't cooked for years one of the children will sometimes ask her what is for supper.

In two of the role-reversal situations (Rebecca and Jack [12], and Carol and Patrick [14]) the children expressed a strong desire to be with their mothers. This served to increase the importance of spending evenings and weekends with them but could also have negative effects on the father. Jack became depressed at his apparent inability to fulfil the role of primary carer because his daughter so clearly wanted Rebecca and cried when she went out to work. It is the influence of the child's wishes that led Kate [1] to divide the care of her first child with her mother and sister rather than use paid child-care. When she tried a child-minder, Ruth was not happy and Kate's mother took her out. Luckily, her sister was available to care for Ruth during the day. Similarly, Alice's [16] desire to dedicate her weekends to the children is reinforced by the children's desire for her to spend more time with them. Sometimes the casting of women in the role of carer appears to come from outside the home. Alice [16] remarks on this in a general way. Lynne and Dave [21] note the influence of social workers on their children's perceptions of both who spends time with them and who *should* spend time with them.

There is another way that the presence of children can influence the division of housework in a living arrangement. The impetus behind some anti-sexist living arrangements is a desire to raise non-sexist/anti-sexist children. One way of influencing children's behaviour is to set an example. Thus for some the division of housework is motivated by a desire to raise children who do not have fixed ideas about women's work and men's work. This was expressed clearly by Carolyn and Roger [15] but many alluded to it in relation to children seeing women doing household maintenance and repairs.

Conclusions

There are differences in the division of housework in my study: from Louise and Mark [8] who seem to accept an unequal division partly because of different standards, to Carolyn and Roger [15] who are trying to overcome the influence of socialization on their standards and abilities. The explicitness of the decision to divide housework equally seems to have some effect here. For some there is a recognition of the oppressive nature of the traditional division of labour and a desire to change this, expressed as the woman not wanting to do what her mother did (e.g. Roseanne [5]) or as a desire to pass on better models to the children (e.g. Carolyn and Roger [15]). For others, the idea of the couple as a partnership of equals leads to a division based on sharing all tasks (e.g. Paula and Rob [17]).

The variety of living arrangements studied highlighted the variety of people dividing a living arrangement's housework. Most studies have looked at couples (usually married/heterosexual with young children); my research not only extends our understandings to different types of living arrangement but also considers the contributions of children and members of other residential groups (paid and unpaid). In this study children of various ages have contributed to housework although not usually on an equal basis. Their contributions will be affected by age to some extent but also by the attitudes of parents to both the compulsion of 'doing chores' and the need to acquire skills, and by the willingness of parents (or other adults) to organize and teach children to do housework. Getting children to do housework may thus increase (at least temporarily) the amount of work to be done.

What is an Anti-sexist Division of Housework?

If, as I allege, the defining characteristic of an anti-sexist living arrangement is the rejection of and resistance to the role/identity of wife, there should be evidence in the division of housework. According to Carole Pateman (1988), the social relations of the public sphere (civil society) are dependent on bodily needs being taken care of in the private sphere for the head of household by his wife (or other dependent). This results in the appropriation of women's paid and unpaid work as documented by Delphy and Leonard (1992). In what way can the living arrangements that I studied be said to be resisting and rejecting these social relations in respect of housework?

Single mothers by choice could be seen to be taking individual responsibility for housework although child-care is often shared with adults outside the residential group, paid and unpaid. Children are encouraged to take responsibility for some tasks. I would not argue that single motherhood is *per se* anti-sexist. Certainly, the argument that many single mothers are doing the same work for the same man without the maintenance (or with less maintenance) and resources as when within marriage is true in many cases[15] (see Delphy and Leonard, 1992, p. 127, fn 6). However, for those in my study who *chose* single motherhood and in many cases had little or no contact with the 'father' of their child(ren) the situation may be different.

The situation of single childless women is perhaps more clearly one of taking individual responsibility for housework primarily by avoiding having communal space whose maintenance would need to be negotiated. Even the two women who were in heterosexual relationships did not do housework for their partners and seemed to divide the few communal activities (primarily social) evenly. The single women in this study, with or without children, are refusing to service men.

In living arrangements with more than one adult (especially couples), I take the *attempt* to arrive at an equal division of housework as evidence of resistance to the responsibility of wives for this work. There is an implicit challenge to the idea that anyone has a right to the services of a wife. This resistance is illustrated, at its most basic level, by Val Peterson's [22] comment that she no longer feels responsible for the housework. In contrast with other studies (e.g. Hochschild, 1989) I did not find evidence of men agreeing to 'help' but still thinking of housework as their wives' responsibility. There was evidence of *struggling* to achieve the goal of equality using a variety of strategies.

Heterosexual couples in role-reversal situations appear to be somewhat of an exception. Except for the gender of the person doing the work, the division of labour in these arrangements is very traditional. In particular the fact that men in these living arrangements are doing the bulk of the housework as well as the child-care is interesting. In most studies role reversals are defined as an exchange of paid work for child-care. Men rarely take on housework and may even limit the extent of child-care (excluding, for example, laundry from its scope) leaving the women with the bulk of the housework in addition to paid work (see Russell, 1987).

Using the theoretical framework outlined in Chapter 1 we can see that in the role reversals of other studies women's labour, paid and unpaid, is appropriated by their husband/partner. Men remain in control of the division of labour — they only do what they want to do — and are still serviced by their wives. In my study participants were explicitly countering the asymmetrical social relations characteristic of the family. Thus a more realistic notion of exchange was introduced. The value placed on mothering as a relationship between adults and children means that men take on housework as well as child-care in order to free women to spend time with the children in the evenings and at weekends. As Delphy and Leonard, and Pateman, point out, the gendered structure remains despite the individual actions of some men, thus it is unlikely that the reversed situation is exploitative of the men in the same way as traditional households are of women. Both men and women in these arrangements are resisting and rejecting the role/identity of 'wife'.

If we consider the strategies of all the participants in the context of Sarah F. Berk's (1985) discovery that housework produces gender as well as household goods and services, we can see that heterosexual couple households have greater hurdles to overcome.[16] Two small studies of lesbian living arrangements also support my conclusions. Both Suzanne Desaulniers (1991) and Helen Peace (1993) treat lesbianism as more than a sexual preference. Studying these living arrangements as anti-sexist, they have found patterns similar to those in my study. In addition, Peace shows that differences in employment status and motherhood do not significantly affect the division of housework in lesbian households.

Men's Commitment

A noticeable difference between the people who took part in my study and those in other studies of working mothers is the commitment of both women *and men* to the goal of equality. The extent of this commitment varied somewhat but many of the beliefs encountered by Arlie Hochschild (1989) and Julia Brannen and Peter Moss (1988, 1991) were completely absent. These two studies both found women believing in their natural suitability for housework and child-care and/or men's inability to do them properly. Perhaps more important is the high incidence, despite the beliefs of women, of men who believed this.

> 40 percent of the women and *three-quarters of the men* in this study did *not* believe in really sharing the responsibility and work of the second shift.
>   (Hochschild, 1989, p. 153; first emphasis added)

Thus these studies concentrate more on how women manage inequalities (emotionally and materially) as well as how they manage differences in ideologies of housework.

The difference between the commitment of the men in my study and the attitudes of the men in these other studies highlights one of the major limitations on the ability to form anti-sexist living arrangements: reliance on men. Men have chosen an egalitarian living arrangement but they can also change their minds. Thus anti-sexist living arrangements are only possible in so far as men are willing to live that way. Men are still heads of household but are using their power to allow a more equal division of labour.

There were several living arrangements in the study which were women only. This included the single mothers by choice, single childless women, and a women-only multiple adult living arrangement.[17] These avoid reliance on men although the social relations which govern their relationships with men outside the residential group (e.g. father of children; heterosexual partner) must be taken into account.

Multiple adult arrangements may also have an advantage over hetero-sexual couple living arrangements in this respect. In these living arrangements the head of household is not so obvious. In particular, where the living arrangement is not focused on a couple or does not contain couples it may start on a more equal footing. However, the structure outlined by Pateman, and Delphy and Leonard affects all cross-gender interaction. Multiple adult living arrangements could also be structured traditionally so that the 'extra' adults were dependants of the head of household in a similar way.

External Contributions

Although children's contribution to housework is a relatively neglected topic, the use of adults outside the residential group is raised in other studies. Brannen and Moss (1988, 1991) point out that this may also add to the total workload as outside help needs to be found and the relationship needs to be maintained.[18] Unpaid help may also have to be reciprocated. However, it is usually seen as reducing the total amount of housework that needs doing (and dividing) within the residential group (Brannen and Moss, 1991, p. 174; Hochschild, 1989, p. 198).

In my study, contributions to housework by adults outside the residential group included both unpaid help from friends and relatives (usually with child-care), and paid help (with child-care and/or cleaning). There were widely divergent practices in the use of full-time paid child-care. While some used child-minders or nurseries (full or part time), a considerable proportion of those in my study wanted to organize their living arrangements so it would not be necessary. Most emphasized that they thought good quality child-care should be available and that women should have the choice but they wanted to raise their children themselves. There were no strong opinions expressed about the use of paid cleaners.

Although no one employs a cook, several living arrangements in my study could be said to have reduced the amount of cooking they do by the indirect employment of someone else. I refer here to the use of convenience foods on a regular basis. For some of the participants (especially the voluntarily childless) eating in restaurants was also a regular occurrence. Issues of both ability and enjoyment seem to enter into the decision-making process in this area. The ability to pay for these options is also important and it seems that voluntarily childless couples are more likely to be able to afford regular restaurant eating than those with children.

The use of outside help (especially paid) raises interesting questions about the type of work people from outside the residential group do, how it is valued, and how people within the residential group make the decision to use them. It also raises broader issues about which living arrangements have the ability to pay for (some) housework and who does housework as paid work.

These issues have been raised elsewhere. Arlie Hochschild questions a resolution of the 'problem' that in effect means devaluing 'the work of caring for [the family]' and accepting male terms of career success (1989, pp. 208–11). Brannen and Moss raise another (perhaps more serious) problem, the polarization of 'career women' and 'domestic workers' (see also Hertz, 1986). Only relatively high-income living arrangements can afford domestic help. Further, the increasing participation of women in paid non-domestic work will reduce the supply of domestic workers thus increasing the price out of most women's range (Brannen and Moss, 1991, p. 259). Others have pointed out that reliance on mothers (and other female relatives) for child-care is dependent on differing labour force participation rates of different groups of women (e.g. Pitrou, 1978, p. 81). Will future generations have their mothers to fall back on?

The focus of most housework research is on the household with these external participants conceptualized as reducing the overall workload (a pattern I have partially reproduced). If we are to have a better understanding of the social relations in which housework is done it may be necessary to develop a more complex model. This is certainly indicated by the proposal that single mothers are still 'wives' to the fathers of their children. Other interesting questions include: are the relations within the residential group being made (apparently) more equal by employing someone else to service the needs of the head of household? Are any of these people being put into the role of wife? What does the analysis of the social relations which obtain in the domestic sphere tell us about the social relations in which paid domestic workers are engaged?

The Way Forward?

Both Hochschild, and Brannen and Moss argue for a comprehensive child-care strategy and improvements to statutory controls on employers enabling parental leave and other 'family friendly' policies. Given the criticisms noted above, housework (other than the child-care provided by nurseries and schools) will also need to be shared if women's 'work-day' is to be reduced. The theoretical framework I have outlined allows us to begin to imagine different social relations in which the tasks necessary to the maintenance of life (or a particular standard of living) might be accomplished in a non-oppressive way. However, Pateman's analysis of the link between the private and public spheres lends support to the view that this will involve much more revolutionary changes in non-domestic work. The issues raised in this chapter regarding the dual nature of child-care and the influence and importance of non-domestic work will be considered in more detail in the next two chapters.

Jo VanEvery

Notes

1   For a brief review of progress and problems see United Nations (1991, p. 90). Marilyn Waring (1989) provides a more pessimistic analysis which suggests that the problems are deeply rooted in the conceptual systems of economics.
2   Gershuny (1983, pp. 145–50) provides a slightly different perspective.
3   Hochschild's (1989) study provides an example of one possibility; Backett's (1982) study of the negotiation of parenting is also illuminating.
4   Numbers in the text and tables refer to the descriptions of the participants in Appendix 1.
5   Karen and Pete [6], all role reversals, Roy and Alice [16], urban collective [19], Petersons [22].
6   In such situations I have avoided the term 'swap' for the sake of clarity and have used 'alternate' instead.
7   It is also partly because she would not do it anyway.
8   Flexibility of non-domestic work will be discussed in more detail in Chapter 5.
9   Alice was living in the house with her two children. Alice and Roy later had two more children.
10   Although a dispute based on environmental concerns it is similar to one based on knowledge, efficiency or standards in that the dispute has been solved by one person taking the responsibility.
11   Jason's active refusal of the 'strategy of needs reduction' noted by Hochschild is evident in the discussion of ironing. Val has offered to iron his shirts but he will not let her.
12   Lisa is considering buying a property with her partner and intends to swap on an equal exchange basis.
13   For a discussion of the absence of equivalence in the traditional family household see Delphy and Leonard (1992, pp. 122–3).
14   The latter is discussed in more detail in Chapter 4.
15   Although as Jan Pahl's research has shown the maintenance of women living with their men cannot be taken for granted either.
16   See especially pp. 203–4 where she discusses the difference between same-sex roommate arrangements and marriage.
17   There was also a lesbian couple with children in the original study.
18   They refer specifically to child-care. On the work of finding a carer see Brannen and Moss (1988, pp. 59–61); on maintaining the relationship (1988, pp. 99–101). See also Hertz (1986, Ch. 5).

Chapter 4

Mothering

Although I included child-care in the discussion of the division of housework, I also noted that the nature of child-care as both work and relationship complicated the analysis. The focus in this chapter will be on the second part of that dual nature. I will look at the importance and practice of mothering[1] amongst the women (and men) in my study — women who are challenging the oppressive nature of 'women's place' in the family.

There are three important themes which emerged from the analysis of the interview material. The first is choice: to have children or not, and to mother them or not. This involves a discussion of the conditions in which women mother or might choose to mother. The second is the balance between mothering and non-domestic work: the practical difficulties of arranging a satisfactory balance, and the importance of both to the identities of individual women (and, sometimes, men).[2] Another interpretation of this theme might be the (relative) importance of mothering. The third theme was support: emotional and practical as well as what might be termed ideological or political support for the choices people had made. Women's choices may also affect the kind and amount of support they get. Although financial support was an issue it will be discussed primarily in Chapter 6.

My focus is clearly on the adults and I discuss mothering from that perspective rather than that of the children. However, some people discussed the importance of children's development as an important motivation and goal of their living arrangement. I will, therefore, include a brief discussion of anti-sexist child-rearing.

Mothering in Sociological and Feminist Research

Many of the studies of housework discussed in Chapter 3 also included aspects of mothering[3] and early feminist writing on mothering was in many ways linked to the writing on housework. Sociological theories (such as those of Parsons) explained women's responsibility for housework as an extension of their mothering role. Early feminist studies focused on the work involved, the isolation, and the disjuncture between women's experience of mothering and its cultural image. In particular, feminism opened up a space in which the negative aspects of mothering could be expressed.[4]

Mothering now appears in feminist and sociological literature in various ways. The work of Nancy Chodorow (1978) on the relationship between women's mothering and women's oppression provided a theoretical account (based on object-relations psychoanalysis) which supported changes in the organization of child-rearing. In particular, Chodorow emphasized the importance of men sharing mothering. Studies such as those of Brannen and Moss (1988, 1991) and Hochschild (1989) demonstrate the rarity of change in this direction. Some feminists have argued that this is because men choose not to mother as an expression of their power (e.g. Polatnick, 1984). Another strand of feminist theorizing celebrates the unique values of mothering and their potential benefit to society if not controlled in a patriarchal institution[5] (e.g. Rich, 1977).

From another perspective research on households and labour markets has concluded that child-care obligations are the most important influence on women's role both at home and in the labour market (e.g. Witherspoon and Prior, 1991, pp. 143–5; Kiernan, 1992, pp. 99–100). Politically, this work has been used in arguments for better child-care provision and more flexible employment (particularly job-sharing and career breaks).

Within the theoretical framework I have been using to make sense of the political actions of the participants in my study, oppressive mothering is seen as related to the work aspect of mothering. Or, more specifically, the social relations in which that work is performed. Mothering as relationship is undertheorized. Miriam Johnson (1988) proposes that mothering, which is based on relations of interdependence, as opposed to dependence and independence, provides a potentially strong basis for the organization of society but is subsumed within the role of wife thus suppressing its potential strength. Delphy and Leonard's (1992) claim that it is men, not children, who appropriate the labour of mothers and Carole Pateman's (1988) exposure of contract theory's reliance on an original story incapable of dealing with relationships with very young children add weight to this conceptualization. All of the formulations reject the idea that mothering is *necessarily* oppressive. Locating women's oppression in the social relations within which they mother allows us to begin to imagine non-oppressive mothering.

Political strategies for transforming mothering have included an under-standing of Chodorow's position as well as a desire to change the material and ideological conditions in which women mother. Shared parenting, public provision of child-care and communal living have all been proposed and fought for. The limits imposed by the structure of employment have also been recognized and questioned: the demand for public child-care is not always linked to women's employment needs. In addition, the ideology of motherhood has been challenged: choice (both to prevent and conceive children) is a key theme of the women's movement. In this chapter I will look at the strategies used by those in my study to transform mothering. How are they rejecting and resisting the role/identity of wife and how far is this transformation possible?

Overview by Arrangement

For women who have chosen to have and raise children on their own, mothering is an important part of their lives. However, all four women would not be satisfied with full-time mothering. Achieving a satisfactory balance between non-domestic work and mothering depended on the sources of practical support primarily in terms of child-care. In terms of political support, some women felt that at least some of the practical and emotional support they had was contingent on downplaying or hiding the deliberate choice of their living arrangement.

Surprisingly the balance between work and motherhood was not important to voluntarily childless heterosexual couples and Pat [24][6] and Lisa [25]. I had expected that the perceived difficulty of achieving a satisfactory balance would have led to a choice between work and motherhood. However, the most common reason for not having children was a dislike of children and/or a lack of a strong desire to mother. Although the idea of choice was not strongly articulated — many made comments like 'I'm not sure if there was a decision really' — it was of primary importance to this group. Political support for their choices was the key issue.

For heterosexual couples in role-reversal situations the issue of choice is linked to the balance between work and mothering. Choosing to have children is related to the importance of looking after them oneself and not using full-time paid child-care. Mothering comes into direct conflict with non-domestic work. For women in this group the primary issues are around the interaction between the roles and identities of worker and mother. For the men, there are more practical issues primarily associated with support and isolation. As we shall see, these are experienced differently by men.

Like the role-reversal situations, the issues surrounding men and mothering are important for heterosexual couples with shared roles. This group differs, however, in that both parents are mothering *and* doing paid non-domestic work. Structural constraints are more in evidence on a daily basis for these couples. The two most important topics in this group are support and the balance between non-domestic work and mothering. Most wanted to take care of their children themselves and also wanted both partners to have an active role in the care of the children. This has not always been possible or easy but is the background against which they talk about mothering.

The multiple adult arrangements are more diverse. Two are what might be termed collectives, the other three are variations on another sort of arrangement. I will therefore discuss them both in terms of the characteristics specific to this category — the existence of more adults — and in relation to the category they most closely resemble. The key issue in this group is support although the balance between non-domestic work and mothering also arises.

Anti-sexist Child-rearing

When Kathryn [28], a lesbian mother, talks about the relative importance of non-domestic work and mothering she links the importance of mothering to 'raising hopefully two boys in a bit of a different way'. This is linked to the importance, expressed by many of the participants, of looking after their children themselves as illustrated by this statement from Liz [10]:

> We took a decision not to have child-minders. My feeling was if we were having children then we would care for them because if they're spending a large part of their day with other people then *they're not learning about how you want them to go about things*.
>
> (Liz, emphasis added)

The purpose of mothering is to raise children, and mothers usually appear in sociological and psychological studies in relation to their children. In the work of Talcott Parsons and others, raising children has been described and analysed as socialization to fit into the society in which they live. Children need to learn acceptable behaviour in order to become adult members of society.[7] Those in my study had a slightly different view of the goals of

Table 4.1: Strategies for anti-sexist child-rearing

	Sex of child	Books, TV, etc.	Toys and games	Clothes	Behaviour	Housework		Questioning
						Doing	Observing	
1	Girls	Not mentioned						
2	Girl	Yes						Yes
3	Boys		Yes	Yes	Yes	Yes		Yes
4	Girl	Yes	Yes	Yes			Yes	
10	Girls	Not mentioned						
11	Boys	Not mentioned						
12	Girl			Yes	Yes			Yes
13	Girls						Yes	
14	Both	Not mentioned						
15	Both						Yes	Yes
16	Both					Yes	Yes	
17	Boy	Yes	Yes					
18	Boy	Not mentioned						
20	Girl						Yes	Yes
21	Both					Yes		Yes
22	Both	Not mentioned						
23	Both	Tries to treat them the same regardless of gender						Yes
28	Boys	Yes	Yes	Yes	Yes	Yes	Yes	Yes

mothering; the work itself was political. Some recognize the effect that their own socialization has had on their ability to live in non-oppressive ways. Most want to raise children who will not conform to the current gendered roles. Their strategies are summarized in Table 4.1. Because the lesbian couple included in the original study used the widest variety of strategies, they have been included as a base-line.

There are two aspects to anti-sexist child-rearing strategies. The first is exposing children to images and behaviours that are not gender stereotyped or that counter gender stereotypes. This can be in books, television shows, clothing and the behaviour of the adults in the living arrangement. The second is to encourage children's independence, including the ability to question things. This often overlaps with the first set of strategies. For example, children can be offered non-sexist books and also encouraged to question the images in both these and other books that they read. Most people used some mix of both.[8]

Strategies around clothing depended on the sex of the child. Girls were helped to make informed choices, often highlighting the impracticality of dresses. Boys were often encouraged to wear 'girls' colours' (e.g. pink, red) or girls' styles (e.g. buckled shoes). The possible effects of children's choices are taken into account by the parents. For example, Ann [3] respects her older son's decision not to wear buckled shoes at school because he gets teased.

Adult behaviour, particularly that related to housework (broadly defined), was often spoken of as setting an example, especially seeing men and women doing a variety of tasks contradicting gender stereotypes. Children were often required to do housework (see Chapter 3 for details) so that they would learn what is involved in running a house. Although anti-sexist child-rearing can involve much more work, raising children to be independent can relieve women of much of the work involved in doing things for them.

Some people, like Ann [3], are ambivalent about how to go about anti-sexist child-rearing. The limits of the strategies outlined above are high-lighted by Carolyn's [15] comment that when their oldest child started school she started talking about nurses as women and doctors as men despite knowing male nurses and women doctors. Ann [3] also recognizes the dilemma of raising boys: How do you encourage assertiveness in boys without risking them misusing it in the traditional male way? She believes that the worst male behaviour is a result of a lack of self-confidence. She feels that if they can be 'quietly confident', they won't need to undermine other people.

Lynne and Dave [21] point out some of the disadvantages of raising children to question and to be independent. Their children will not accept authority without a reason which has caused problems at school, with their friends' parents and when their oldest daughter left home.

Jo: At least they won't get trod upon.
Lynne: But they don't fit with the world and that's a problem, you know, negotiating them into the world. If you don't fit the world to some extent you've actually ... they have to negotiate with the world.
Jo: So you've kind of raised kids for a world that doesn't exist?
Lynne: In some ways. In other ways. ... Yeah to a certain extent yes it's not ... the kids aren't within the family for the rest of their lives. They have to get out there. ...

Lynne is not clear that the way they raised them was entirely positive.

As my study focuses on the position of women and how that might change, I do not have the information or the expertise to evaluate the effectiveness of these strategies for raising anti-sexist (or non-sexist) children. However, they do affect the position of women, and may also be one of the reasons for transforming the relationships between the adults in the living arrangement.[9]

Choice

In her review of feminist debates around mothering, Sheila Rowbotham (1989b) points out that although early feminist statements were seen to be anti-mothering, they must be understood in the context of 1960s social values. Those statements challenged the idea that women's happiness could come only from motherhood and opened up a space in which the depressing and violent feelings of mothers could be expressed. Rowbotham stresses that the overall feminist position was one of choice — to be or not to be a mother — which included examining the reasons behind either choice.[10]

The issue of choice in feminism is most obvious in the struggles about safe, effective contraception and abortion. Technological advances in reproductive technologies are now extending 'woman's right to choose' beyond previous biological limits (Stanworth, 1987). However, as Sue Himmelweit (1988) points out, we need to look not only at the choices of individual women but also at the conditions in which those choices are made. Diane Richardson (1993, pp. 62–86) discusses the issues involved in detail.

Richardson argues that technological advances are not sufficient to give women reproductive choice especially since access to many of them is controlled by men. In addition, many women's choices are limited by their relatively powerless position in heterosexual relations. Condoms might be a safe, effective method of contraception which also prevents disease but a woman cannot choose this method if her male partner will not wear one!

The issue of choice must also be considered in relation to the pressures on women to have children. Although mothering is relatively undertheorized by Pateman, Johnson, and Delphy and Leonard, the framework I have developed from their work indicates that, as wives, women are required to bear and rear children for the head of household. Children are necessary for the transmission function of the family.[11] Miriam Johnson draws our attention to the way that motherhood is constructed as a desire in women. West and Zimmerman's notion of 'accountability' implies that mothering is, perhaps, an accountable womanly activity which could legitimize other activities (1987, p. 136). The compulsion to mother does not preclude women's desire to mother in *different* ways or their efforts to transform mothering.

My use of the term 'mothering' requires the analytical separation of mothering as a nurturing activity from the physical/biological processes of conception and childbirth. When Johnson talks of the libratory potential of mothering it is to the former that she refers. Both aspects of mothering are evident in the living arrangements studied. I distinguish them by using the term 'having children' for the latter.

Single Mothers by Choice

For most women in this category the choice to mother is not separated from the choice to have children. The decision to continue with an accidental pregnancy or to arrange conception is a choice to mother. For example, when Kate became pregnant accidentally about six years ago she decided that she did not have the financial and emotional resources to mother another child and terminated her pregnancy. These women also made positive choices to mother as single parents. For those who made their choices prior to conception, this involved working out how to conceive and yet maintain one's single parent status. The issues surrounding their decisions are summarized in Table 4.2.

Jane's [4] situation illustrates the complicated nature of the choice to mother and the possibility of separating it from the choice to give birth to a child. As a child and adolescent she had an ambivalent attitude to potential motherhood but if she was to mother would want to do it when relatively young and as a single parent. In Jane's second year of university she started to want a child by her long-term heterosexual partner. She began having 'accidents' — being careless with her contraception.[12] Initially she was not taking responsibility for what she was doing but eventually resolved the contradictions she felt between wanting a baby and 'using' her partner.[13] Jane began trying in earnest to get pregnant (calculating dates, etc.) but it never seemed to work out.

Around this time she also started a sexual relationship with another man.[14] Although he had made it clear that he was not interested in unprotected sex, Jane was confidently using the rhythm method with the diaphragm. Her desire for her long-term partner's child was now overridden by her desire for *a* child and she 'forgot' to use the diaphragm during her unsafe period. She had not really 'planned' to get pregnant but rather 'not prevented' it. Although the following day she wrote in her diary that she was pregnant, she forgot about it completely, even explaining away her late period with exam stress.

When the pregnancy was confirmed she treated it as one would an accidental pregnancy. She decided not to have an abortion but her decision

Table 4.2: The choices of single mothers

Name	Conception		Influences on decision	Benefits	Drawbacks
	Accidental	Planned			
1 Kate — 1st child	One-night stand with friend		Support of family and friends	Focus on kids over couple; stability (cf. divorce)	Not mentioned
2nd child		Fling with barman while on holiday	Belief that 'family' includes siblings; negative — money		
2 Maggie	Ex-boyfriend who didn't want responsibility		Regretted childlessness on divorce; advice of friend; article in magazine	No negative aspects of couple relationship; more likely to get external support	Money, loneliness, anxiety
3 Ann (both)	In a relationship with their father (not cohabiting)		Single mother friend; support of commune	Stability	Unspecified
4 Jane		Planned to get pregnant by long-term partner, accidentally by another man (see discussion)	Early rejection of marriage; wanted something out of relationship	No negatives of couple	Unspecified

to mother came later. Jane remained open to adoption even after the birth and only decided to mother when she picked the baby up from her mother's after her exams. Dorothy was three months old.

The women in this category were making positive choices to mother without being/becoming wives. Not only are most of the pregnancies planned but most of the women have little or no contact with their child(ren)'s father. They also cite the absence of a couple relationship as an advantage of their situation. Although all have had short relationships since the birth of their children, none of the women in this category wishes to be in a long-term couple relationship.

Voluntarily Childless

Most of those in voluntarily childless heterosexual couples had remained childless because they didn't like children. Roseanne [5] expressed this view particularly strongly. Although she likes children, Louise [8] is indifferent to having any of her own perhaps because of her earlier responsibilities for the care of her (six) younger siblings, the youngest of whom had Down's Syndrome and needed a lot of attention. Only Barbara and Juan [9] mentioned negative reactions to this decision in the form of people saying that they would change their minds when they got older. The men seem to have thought about it (and talk about it) less than the women. Pete [6] can see from some of his work colleagues the possibility of being a 'part-time' father and disapproves of the way that the decision to have children is left to women. Unlike the women in the voluntarily childless heterosexual couples, both Pat [24] and Lisa [25] talk about their decisions not to mother as being retaken several times usually in relation to external expectations associated with marriage.

Peg [7] and Lisa [25] are the only people in this group who really enjoy children. Peg is in contact with them through her work as a health visitor, is very supportive of her sister (a single mother), and most of her friends have children. Peg has never desired children of her own, a feeling reinforced by her beliefs, influenced by radical feminism, that having children changes the balance of power in a heterosexual relationship to the disadvantage of women. She comments that her sister's situation is probably preferable. Lisa also says that she 'share[s] other people's' children and has contact with children through her work as a teacher.

As Richardson (1993, pp. 63–74) points out, the choice to remain childless can be a difficult one particularly for married, heterosexual women. Control over fertility requires access to contraceptive technologies (often mediated by doctors and/or men) and control over sexual practice. Socially it may mean contradicting accepted constructions of femininity (which include a mothering component) and having other activities on which to base one's adult identity.

Heterosexual Couples with Children in Role-reversal Situations

In this category the men are the primary carers; the women, the 'bread-winners'. Only one woman talks about her choice as one of whether or not to have children: Carol's [10] decision is clearly not to mother. Had Patrick not offered to be the primary carer, she probably would never have had children. The other women have made choices which are related to the balance between work and mothering (discussed further below). The influences on their choices are presented in Table 4.3. Although they have not chosen not to mother, as evidenced by the importance of spending time with the children in the evenings and at weekends (see Chapter 3) they have chosen to mother in a different way.

The men in this group were making unusually strong choices to mother. They had all given up full-time paid employment and become primary carers. Not only does this provide the conditions in which the women could make their choices, it is also important in itself. Another important factor is that all

Table 4.3: The choice to reverse roles

	Non-domestic work when decision made		Other influences
	Woman	Man	
10	Recently qualified social worker	Recently redundant	Belief that equally capable
11	Accountant, career disrupted by move to England	Executive of computer firm	Wilhelm always envisaged taking time out
12	Librarian	Writing music (unpaid)	Re-evaluation of financial constraints
13	Secretary	Wanted to devote more time to political activism	Dan always very involved; had reversed roles in a previous relationship; Linda found combining work and mothering stressful
14	Civil servant	'High flyer' management trainee	Carol had 'propagation urge' after father's death; Patrick disliked his work

the women believe that men are equally capable of mothering. This is in stark contrast with the results of other studies (e.g. Hochschild, 1989; Brannen and Moss, 1991) which demonstrate the extent of beliefs to the contrary.

I received a letter which demonstrates (by contrast) the importance of this belief. Lucy [26], who describes her attempt at a role reversal as 'an exhausting failure', talks about how she deeply mistrusted anyone else's ability to look after her child properly and felt that practical things, like changing nappies, were not getting done often enough. She also worried about the baby's safety. Consequently in the evenings and at weekends Lucy felt a desire to 'grab back the baby [she] had missed so much at work'. Her own deep-seated emotions and beliefs about mothering had a very real effect on her ability to choose a different arrangement for herself.

With the exception of Carol the decision to have children remains largely unexamined in this category. What is interesting, especially given societal prescriptions of masculinity,[15] is the fact that the men are so willing to give up non-domestic work as their primary activity and source of identity and take on mothering, and that the women accept this possibility. This allows women to achieve some sort of balance between non-domestic work and mothering.

Heterosexual Couples with Children with Shared Roles

The issues in this category are similar to the role-reversal category. The difference is partly one of degree: the balance between work and mothering is more even for both men and women. However, there is also a more fundamental questioning of the traditional division of domestic and non-domestic work between members of a living arrangement. There is no identifiable primary carer or primary earner.

Although their relationship to paid work differs from that of the men in role reversals, the men in shared-role living arrangements still have an extraordinary commitment to mothering. For Eric [18] this is conditioned by past experience; for Rob [17], by his view of marriage as a partnership; and for Roger [15] and Roy [16] by their commitment to feminist politics.

None of the women talks about the decision whether or not to have children. Jean [18] is the only person in this group to mention it (she has always wanted children and wants another) but doesn't question this desire in any way. When Jeremy [17] was born Paula discovered that she doesn't like babies very much illustrating the 'taken for granted' nature of mothering even among women who question other aspects of women's position.

Multiple Adult Arrangements

Like the heterosexual couples with children, there is little discussion of the decision to have children in this category. There are only children in four of these living arrangements and in two (the Petersons [22] and Mary [23]), the birth of children significantly predates the explicit anti-sexist character of the living arrangement. In the urban collective [19], Laura is now trying to have a child, a decision she relates to the rather new (biological) possibility following the solution of a prolonged medical problem.

Lynne's [21] oldest child was born when she was in a relationship in which she was often the main breadwinner and her ex-husband took on substantial amounts of child-care and housework. The youngest and the three foster children pre-date their role reversal although there was never any question of Dave not being involved. There was a definite role reversal when Lynne started her degree course. Because of the foster children the initial choice was not final. When the youngest foster child reached the 'teenage bit' Lynne and Dave decided that they couldn't cope with it so they had social services place her with another family. Dave, who was the primary carer, says that, although it may be unacceptable, they are tired. They gave it a 'real ten year blast' and now he wants some 'me time'. They were not prepared to go through it again without any support.

Miriam's [20] situation is similar to that of the single mothers by choice. Becki was planned and born while Miriam was married; she left her husband within a year of her daughter's birth. Although she had been aware of (and dissatisfied with) the roles she and her husband took on, the arrival of the baby brought into sharp relief the power relationship in her marriage and she chose not to mother in those conditions. The advantages of her living arrangement are the informal support and the lack of gender battles in the house.

Of those in the rural collective [23] Sara talks about mothering and both the benefits of collective living (particularly for Mary) and her choice to remain childless.

> I've never had kids of my own and I think ... all along I just feel motherhood is so undervalued and under-rated. This society just does not acknowledge what mothers do.
>
> (Sara)

Choosing the conditions in which to mother is important in this category. The support and financial benefits of multiple adult arrangements open up possibilities not available to women (and men) in other categories. Lynne and Dave's [21] decision to stop mothering is indicative of the importance of support.

The Politics of Choice

Amy and Kathryn [28], a lesbian couple with children, discussed the difference between heterosexual women and lesbians in terms of choice and children. This sheds light on the lack of discussion amongst women in heterosexual couples in this study. Amy and Kathryn believe that it is so difficult for lesbians to have children that they really want them and have thought it out really thoroughly. For heterosexual women it is much easier (and can even happen accidentally) which gives mothering a different status.

> I think we've also tried to — I mean 'we' and women who have made very positive decisions, with a lot of support, to have children — have actually tried to redefine what motherhood is and the fact that it needn't be oppressive, it needn't be miserable, boring, etc. The sharing of the housework, the sharing of the money, the sharing of paid work and motherhood and everything else, demanding a bit of respect from the children and respecting them as people means that motherhood's been redefined. And I find motherhood wonderful. And so do other women that I know who've chosen, as we have, to do it in a very different way, have found it wonderful. A really wonderful experience to go through. So hopefully that experience can be sort of passed on to try to make motherhood something where you don't have to be so self-sacrificing and powerless and all that sort of thing as my mother found it.
>
> (Kathryn)

Choice was an important issue mainly in the negative — the ability of women in heterosexual couples to choose not to have children. This is perhaps inherent in this sort of political action. It is much easier to reject a societal expectation than to give it new meaning. Positive choices were made only by those who would not normally be expected to mother: lesbians and single women. The benefits of single motherhood, according to those in my study, included stability and the ability to focus on themselves and the children without the drawbacks of a couple relationship, thus highlighting the separation of the roles/identities of wife and mother.

Women in heterosexual couples with children had not questioned motherhood (with the exception of Carol [14]) and thus could not be said to have made a positive choice to mother. Indeed many talked about the importance of the anti-sexist living arrangement in terms of their children. This could be seen as but a modification of traditional motherhood in which women's roles/identities are defined in relation to others. Their transformation of motherhood is perhaps more clearly located in the redefinition of the balance between non-domestic work and mothering.

The Balance between Mothering and Non-domestic Work

The issue of striking a balance between non-domestic work and mothering highlights the fact that within the family system mothering is elided with housework and women's domestic role/identity (including mothering) is prioritized over any possible non-domestic role/identity. Women as wives fit their non-domestic work around their domestic responsibilities. The vast majority of mothers of pre-school children do not take paid work or work only part-time (Kiernan, 1992). That it is the role/identity of *wife*, and not mother, that is key to this prioritization of the domestic is evidenced by the early appearance of this pattern in married couples (see Mansfield and Collard, 1988, pp. 120–37). In a more theoretical context, Delphy and Leonard (1992) state that one way men control their wives' participation in paid work is by permitting it on the condition that their domestic work does not suffer. The increased domestic workload associated with young children may thus account for the way this often appears in the statistical evidence as an effect of being a mother. Participants in my study varied in the priority given to domestic and non-domestic roles/identities but most challenged the traditional pattern to some extent.

The balance between work and mothering was raised in different ways in different categories. For some, particularly single mothers, it was closely linked with the issue of support. For others, it was discussed in terms of practical arrangements between adult members of a living arrangement. For men, cultural constructions of masculinity stress the importance of non-domestic, paid work and reject nurturing behaviour as feminine. Men in my study often raised the issue of balance in terms of their choice to mother. Some of the issues raised in this section will be discussed in more detail in the following chapter; in particular the issues of the relationship between non-domestic work and identity, and the flexibility of non-domestic work.

Jane [4] was the only one of the single mothers by choice engaged in full-time mothering although this was not ideal. Benefit constraints were the primary reason. She does have some non-domestic interests, primarily artistic, which occasionally bring in money. Of the other three women, Ann [3] was working part time, Maggie [2] full time and Kate [1] freelance. Kate [1] referred to someone's comment on her arrangement that she 'couldn't enjoy the children without the work but wouldn't enjoy the work without the children'. This seems to sum up the attitude of all the single mothers. None of these women finds mothering fulfilling in itself but it is one important role and identity for them.

When I started this project my expectation of the voluntarily childless couples was that they might have chosen childlessness because of the difficulties of being both mothers and workers. This was not confirmed by my research. Women in this category were not dissatisfied with the options regarding the balance between work and mothering, they had no desire to mother.

Only one of the couples (Karen and Pete [6]) mentioned balance and then only as a secondary point. Karen is critical of the conditions in which she would mother in this society. She also believes, based on the experience of a friend, that her work as a writer would not mix well with mothering. She would be very unhappy if she couldn't write. Pete is well aware, unlike other people in this category, of some of the structural reasons why most of his work colleagues are childless. The nature of his job as a computer consultant and the organizational structure make it difficult for people to have children.

The balance between non-domestic work and mothering has been considered by both Pat [24] and Lisa [25] at various times although their original disinterest in motherhood provides the context for their decisions. Pat says of the fact that she would have to work full-time to afford a child, 'it just gets cock-eyed'. When the issue of children came up early in Lisa's marriage, she believed that one should stay home for the first five years but didn't want to give up her career.

For those in role reversals the balance between work and mothering resembles that of the conventional nuclear family household. For the women the balance is weighted towards non-domestic work; for the men, towards mothering. There is a strong feeling about not having full-time paid child-care. Some women, like Rebecca [12], are unsatisfied with the balance and would prefer to spend more time with their children. Others are happy with their situation. Linda [13] found it quite difficult to adjust to the change of circumstances although Dan had always been involved in their children's care. She describes the change in terms of her identity: she had always put 'mother' quite high on the list of what she was but doesn't now.

The men are all satisfied with their balance although the desire of children to spend time with their mothers can have negative effects. This was most pronounced for Jack [12]. Dan [13] had taken mothering further, working as a child-minder when the children were younger. He says, 'The job is to deal with the kids, bring 'em on, develop 'em and that's worthwhile business, isn't it?' Although his satisfaction does not come solely from mothering, he values mothering and politics over paid non-domestic work.

Wilhelm and Christiane [11] are in a more complicated position. Christiane's ideas about the balance between work and mothering have changed over time as her circumstances have changed. Earlier in life she had always prioritized mothering and assumed that she would not work outside the home when her children were young. She then discovered that she enjoyed her work so decided to put off child-bearing. The move to England changed things. Christiane stayed at home full time for two years when the children were very young. The part-time solution that they would both prefer has not been possible but Wilhelm was able to negotiate a 16-month unpaid leave of absence so that Christiane could pursue her career.

The women in role reversals made the kinds of choices about mothering and work that I expected from the voluntarily childless. Because their partners were willing to take on the primary responsibility for mothering they were able to sidestep a pure choice between work and mothering. The men have made the unusual choice of not doing full-time paid non-domestic work.

Unlike the couples in role-reversal situations, the couples with shared roles are trying to enable both partners to have a more or less even balance between non-domestic work and mothering. Two couples have managed rather well although it hasn't been easy either practically or emotionally. The other two have been constrained by their inability to find suitable non-domestic work. The men in this category are similar to those who are primary carers in that they reject the societal prescription of full-time paid work for men.

Both Paula [17] and Alice [16] feel guilty about not spending enough time with their children. This is exacerbated for Paula because the provision of activities *with* children is not designed for working women. For both of these women, their partners are also mothering. This has both positive and negative effects. Work, family and politics are equally important to Roy [16]. Alice has taken a full-time job but rates very highly the importance of the children being able to come home from school most days, and wishes Roy to continue working part time. In contrast Paula's [17] guilt feelings are exacerbated by her perception that Rob has a stronger relationship with Jeremy than she does.

Jean and Eric [18] both work freelance and have had few problems organizing the fit between mothering and work. Mothering is important to Jean but she thinks that work takes priority over mothering. Eric is not as satisfied with his balance. He would prefer to be in a role reversal. In contrast, external constraints have frustrated Carolyn and Roger [15]. They stress mothering as more important and would like to strike a balance in which both of them can take a strong mothering role and divide the non-domestic work necessary to finance their living arrangement more or less equally. They have had problems achieving this and Carolyn has often been depressed and angry.

For heterosexual couples with children the balance between work and mothering for each partner is heavily dependent on that pursued by the other partner as well as on external conditions (like the availability of flexible work). In the multiple adult arrangements this is not necessarily the case. The availability of support from other members of the arrangement and the financial benefits of living in a larger residential group contribute to women's ability to find a suitable balance between non-domestic work and mothering.

Dave was the only man in this category for whom this theme was relevant. Although Lynne and Dave's [21] arrangement resembles a role-reversal situation, Lynne's balance between work and mothering is similar to that of the women in heterosexual couples with shared roles. Her job as a researcher is quite flexible and she often works from home. Dave's rejection of full-time paid work is similar to the other men in the study. He has struck a balance between mothering and his various non-domestic activities with paid work given relatively low priority.

The financial benefits of a multiple adult arrangement allow Miriam [20] to pursue a satisfactory balance between work and mothering now endangered by the breakdown of the co-ownership arrangement. The importance of mothering to Mary [23] is evident in her decision to give up a stressful job, but she implies that were the conditions better she would like to be able to do both. This must be seen in the context of the support she was getting from other members of the rural collective which allowed her to maintain an identity separate from the children.

What is considered a satisfactory balance between non-domestic work and mothering varies among those who took part in the study. None of the women would be satisfied with full-time mothering but some have been more successful than others at reaching a suitable balance. Some women would also not be satisfied with full-time non-domestic work although the voluntarily childless women and some of those in role-reversal situations are. The situations of the men are more varied. Although some are happy with full-time non-domestic work and little or no involvement in mothering, others are trying to strike a balance between the two. The men in the role-reversal situations prefer a balance more heavily weighted towards mothering. The advantage of multiple adult arrangements in this respect is the lower dependence on one other person's balance in order to reach a satisfactory balance for oneself. The disadvantage of single motherhood is the dependence on people outside their living arrangements (often paid).

It is in this balance that the anti-sexist nature of the role reversal is most obvious. Although it is not clear that women in these living arrangements have made positive choices to have children, they have clearly given greater priority to non-domestic work. This is most obvious in Carol's [14] case as she would not have had children in any other circumstance. These arrangements were also least critical of the organization of the capitalist economic system in that they accepted the full-time, committed nature of work in that system. Some would have preferred a different organization of non-domestic work, similar to that reached by many of the single mothers and those in heterosexual couples with shared roles. These latter arrangements were more directly in conflict with the organization of work in the capitalist economy and more constrained by it.

Support

Early feminist writing highlighted some of the negative aspects of mothering in western capitalist societies. The depression and violent feelings that some women were feeling were partly a result of the isolated conditions in which mothering often takes place. The solution was seen in supporting motherhood in various ways. Issues of support were crucial for the people that I interviewed.

One type of support is practical. As we have seen in the previous section, the women in my study were dependent on practical support (from their partners, other people they might live with and people outside the residential group) for child-care, both formal and informal. Emotional support came from much the same places but was also found amongst women (and men) in similar situations. Men who choose to mother often feel isolated because they do not blend easily into mothers' traditional support structures.

The third form of support is political. Transforming mothering often means losing the support of the community. Many women face accusations, both implicit and explicit, that they are 'unfit' or inadequate mothers. For some people in my study this resulted in a new kind of isolation. For others, new communities of support were formed.

Single Mothers by Choice

Support is crucial for single mothers who want to achieve a satisfactory balance between non-domestic work and mothering. The situations of these women illustrate the multiplicity of possible sources of support both

Table 4.4: *Support for single mothers*

	Practical and emotional		Political	
	Mother, sisters	Friends, neighbours	Positive	Negative
1	Lots incl. regular child-care	Lived with friend early on	Many friends who are single mothers	Very little
2	Back-up practical; emotional	Holidays and weekend activities with friends		Doesn't know any single parents
3		Commune early on; has shared flats; father of child (practical)	Same as practical	Media, political statements
4	Mother not close (physically or emotionally)	Maintained only one friend locally; isolated on council estate		Pressure from university when pregnant

emotional and practical. The issue of financial support, although not discussed explicitly here, has an impact. In order to afford paid child-care[16] a certain income is necessary. Given the political climate, support for their choices is also important. Both Maggie [2] and Jane [4] mention that the most common misunderstanding of their situations is that their pregnancies were accidental and they were abandoned. Their desire to correct this impression of them as victims is counteracted by the perception that they would get less support if they emphasized that their situations were deliberate.[17] The support they received is presented in Table 4.4.

Jane's [4] isolation has contributed to her dissatisfaction with full-time mothering. She believes that her lack of support is related to her identity being primarily as a single woman not as a mother. The practical assistance and emotional support that Kate [1] has had have enabled her to support herself financially and to enjoy mothering. Ann [3] prefers a more continuously negotiated sharing to an assumption that everything will be shared all the time (which is what she experienced in the commune). Maggie's [2] lack of contact with other single mothers reinforces her impression that she is going against the grain and lives in a 'couples' world'.

Voluntarily Childless

The voluntarily childless had surprisingly little negative reaction to their choice. Most of the couples socialize and work with other childless people.

Peg [7] is the exception, socializing during the day (meeting for lunch) and at people's houses so that they don't need baby-sitters. It is interesting that any reaction they do get is in relation to their neglect of 'wifely' duties rather than their refusal to mother (see Chapter 2). Karen's [6] mother has accepted her childlessness but has reacted negatively to her dislike of babies, which Karen suspects she thinks is unfeminine, and her failure to 'look after' Pete. Peg's [7] clients' assumption that her childlessness is because she is a 'career woman' indicate that perhaps it has become acceptable to choose work over motherhood.

Lisa's [25] situation illustrates the importance of support for those who have decided to remain childless. She is a member of three women's groups. In two of these all but Lisa and one other woman have children and take the attitude that the childless women 'wouldn't understand' about mothering. She finds the third group, made up solely of childless women, more supportive.

Heterosexual Couples with Children in Role-reversal Situations

The women in role reversals have not had negative reactions to their choice of non-domestic work as their primary role[18] although Carol [14] initially detected some resentment from her friends that she could combine a career, children and a sound marriage, and Christiane's [11] mother thinks that she is being deprived of her children. Two of the women in this category were primary carers before their current arrangement. Christiane stayed home full time for two years but, in order to counter her potential isolation in a new country, they had an *au pair*. She speculates that had she still been in Europe she would have relied on friends for support instead. When Linda [13] had responsibility for the children she had no support other than paid child-minders and her employer is not very flexible about time off for family responsibilities.

The issue of support is primarily related to men's involvement in mothering. The traditional sources of women's support are not accessible in a straightforward way, although some men seem to have more difficulties than others. This is often explained in terms of their personalities, describing themselves as 'not a joiner' (Jack [12]) or 'not bothered being a nobody in this context' (Wilhelm [11]). Steve [10] has not felt completely out of place amongst the women in the neighbourhood or walking the children to school and has never met with purposeful exclusion. He is involved in playgroup and school activities and sometimes watches the neighbour's children while she goes into town. However, he recognizes that perceptions of masculine sexuality may affect men's ability to participate in some activities. He thinks there is probably a sexual connotation to inviting him in for coffee and speculates whether some of the husbands are suspicious. Of the few people who did invite him one was a grandmother whose age, presumably, would counteract any possible sexualization of the relationship by others.

Rebecca and Jack [12] moved into the city to counter the isolation he felt when their daughter was very young. Although he doesn't have a lot of contact with other mothers, Jack has one close friend amongst them, is on the playgroup committee, and now gets practical support from his mother and sister-in-law. Patrick [14] was the treasurer of the playgroup and the nanny next door invites him round for coffee. They now get practical support from Carol's sister who sometimes has the children for the weekend. Dan [13] is involved in activities at the school like stage managing the school play.

The issue of political support seems to be one of the sexual connotations of men's caring. Both Liz [10] and Jack [12] worried about the public perception of the child abuse problem and whether it would affect men's ability to have other children in their homes. Fortunately this has not been a problem. Rebecca [12] is the only woman in this category to mention political support. She is a member of the local Working Mothers Association but notes that, while she would prefer a more campaigning role, it seems to be mostly a social network. Many of the members are women in dual-career couples with high incomes who employ full-time nannies.

Heterosexual Couples with Children with Shared Roles

Although men in this category experience problems similar to those of men in role reversals with regard to traditional sources of support in the community it doesn't seem to be as central an issue for them. Perhaps this is because their lives are not as focused on mothering as an activity and identity. However, for women, negotiating the balance between work and mothering seems to require more support than a role reversal. Political support seems to be directly related to practical and emotional support. There is also more discussion of support in terms of the couple.

Paula and Rob [17] were involved in setting up a Working Parents Association[19] and this has reduced their isolation in the community. Paula [17] and Jean [18] are both frustrated by the lack of emotional support given to them compared with their husbands. The men are asked how they are coping with the baby (which the women are not, even though they feel that their husbands are more experienced). Jean says people only ask her how she is coping with the baby *and work.*

Table 4.5: Support for heterosexual couples with children with shared roles

	Practical and emotional		Political	
	Relatives	Friends, neighbours	Positive	Negative
15		Mother-and-toddler groups 'strange' for Roger; like-minded friends		No public support for men as mothers; child-care as 'women's issue'
16	Some practical	Older friend	Political colleagues	
17	No	Working Parents' Association	Working Parents' Association	Different beliefs from women in mother-and-toddler groups and church; Rob isolated in mother-and-toddler activities
18	Some practical	Like-minded friends in area	Eric in organization for fathers; like-minded friends	

The isolation of men in the community of mothers is again an issue. Roger and Carolyn [15] are unable to articulate why he feels strange in mother-and-toddler groups especially as he generally prefers the company of women. Paula and Rob [17] talk about the isolation of men in mother-and-toddler activities in terms of Jeremy's loss of an opportunity to play with the other children after the structured activity.

In this category practical support comes primarily from the other partner although Paula and Rob [17] use paid child-care and Roy and Alice [16] have the support of a friend. The difficulties are largely in terms of political support for their choices and, for women, the recognition that they may not be able to 'cope' with their children.

Multiple Adult Arrangements

One of the advantages of this type of arrangement is live-in support. Because both Jason and Margaret [22] were there, Val never felt any guilt about leaving the children. Lynne and Dave [21] had the emotional support of friends who lived with them when their children were teenagers. Their teenagers were difficult and three of the children were going through adolescence at the same time.

Because of the foster children Lynne and Dave have had a lot of social work involvement in their lives but social workers have not provided the support they needed. They feel that the social workers tended to reinforce traditional ideas of appropriate roles although not always explicitly.

> Things don't even have to be said at all but the quality and the strength that they can come over underlying can be ferociously strong and we might not be able to even verbalize it, you know. It's nice when those things aren't privatized because they make so much more sense and are easier to work with but it's all very private, isn't it, and hidden all that stuff.
>
> (Dave)

Dave has found his role difficult at times particularly in terms of having friendships with men. Because of his involvement with the children, most of the adults he was meeting were women. He did make some friends and often felt fine in that situation but sometimes felt uncomfortable. Dave made a conscious effort to meet men and became involved in a Fathers' Network, mainly composed of fathers staying at home or trying to right the balance a bit, which ran playgroups and other things.

In terms of societal expectations and what I have called political support, Lynne feels that in their situation she comes across as selfish. Lynne's exposure to feminism has helped her understanding of the tensions involved, leading to more satisfaction with the balance between being a wife/mother and doing other things. The reactions Dave gets reinforce the unusual nature of men mothering — progressive friends emphasize how wonderful he is; his parents think he's a 'poof'.[20]

Miriam [20] has primary responsibility for Becki but others in the house will informally take her out to places or baby-sit. She also has a reciprocal baby-sitting arrangement with a neighbour one night a week. Sara [23] states that the most important reason they responded to my request for participants was to do with the way they have combined Mary's primary responsibility for the children with others taking part in their care and allowing her some space separate from them. Not all of the members of the rural collective have been supportive but they are an important source of support. In addition Mary has made some friends, through the children, in the nearby village although it is rather insular and difficult for outsiders.

Support for Anti-sexist Mothering

Practical and emotional support came from a variety of sources including traditional ones (e.g. mothers, sisters, partners) and wider networks of friends, playgroups and organizations. The problems of practical and emotional support are reduced when living in multiple adult arrangements. For those challenging traditional roles, political support can be particularly important enabling them to counter the values of their parents, politicians and the media. Some of the participants formed their own organizations to this end (e.g. Paula and Rob [17]). However, Dave's [21] experience left him feeling cynical about the prospects for change. Many of the men involved in the Fathers' Network reverted to old patterns when their children got older.

The balance between autonomy and support is difficult to maintain. Lynne's [21] articulation of the perceptions of role reversals and the comments that Jean [18] and Paula [17] got regarding 'coping' highlight the ways in which the family system is maintained and enforced.[21] The comments of some women living without men that support was often dependent on playing down the deliberate choice of unmarried motherhood also illustrates the enforcement of the merger of wife and mother.

Conclusions

The way that the participants in my study are transforming mothering may indicate the important elements of a theory of the social relations in which mothering normally occurs. The first is related to choice. The lack of evidence of positive choices to mother amongst the women in heterosexual couples indicates the depth of the connection between femininity and motherhood. The work of Miriam Johnson and that of Nancy Chodorow indicate that psychological and psychoanalytic theories might be useful to understand women's 'choice' of motherhood despite its negative aspects. The choices made by single women and lesbians, and the voluntarily childless indicate efforts to separate mothering from the role/identity of wife. The difficulties of reconciling this political action with getting the necessary support indicate the ways that conventional roles are enforced. My theoretical framework also renders the negative reactions of the parents/siblings of the voluntarily childless women (to their unwifely behaviour) less peculiar.

The transformation of mothering and the attempt to change the social relations in which women mother is only possible in so far as suitable non-domestic work is available and one can get the required support without becoming a wife. The first will be discussed in detail in the next chapter. As for the second, again (as for the division of housework) women are dependent on men's choices or their ability to live without men.

Men Mothering

Studies of fatherhood have shown that, despite a rhetoric of greater paternal involvement and even equality in child-rearing, mothers are still doing much more of the work (Lewis and O'Brien, 1987a). In this context the men with children in my study are exceptional. This is true for both those in role reversals and for those in relationships with shared roles. Even in comparison with studies of men in role reversals, those in my study go much further in their challenge to traditional paternal roles. It is evident that the tendency of men in my study to take over responsibility for housework as well as child-care is rare.[22]

One key issue is the acceptance by both the men and the women of the ability of men to mother. For example, Backett notes that mothers in her study were perceived as being more knowledgeable about the child's needs (1987, p. 77). This is in sharp contrast with Paula and Rob [17], a heterosexual couple with shared roles, who felt that Rob was more knowledgeable about Jeremy's needs. However, this knowledge was gained in ways similar to the women in Backett's study — Rob had more contact with the baby. Brannen and Moss (1991, p. 85) found a similar attitude in their study and also provide evidence from the British Social Attitudes survey supporting the general acceptance of the view that women are better able to mother than men (1991, p. 93). Acceptance of men's ability to mother has also been cited as an important antecedent of role reversal (Russell, 1987, p. 165), and has been related to the nature of shared child-care arrangements (Coltrane, 1989).

However, comparable information is difficult to find. In Kathleen Kiernan's contribution to the 1992 report of the British Social Attitudes survey only attitudes to *women* working and the family life cycle are analysed, and questions about housework include only two child-care tasks, one of which is intermittent (Kiernan, 1992). Questions about flexible work and child-care arrangements in the 1991 report assume women's responsibility for children thus preventing any assessment of men's involvement[23] (Witherspoon and Prior, 1991).

The situations of the men in my study indicate some of the constraints on men taking a more active parental role. Although some men have found it easier than others, most have encountered difficulties in gaining access to traditional sources of mothers' support in communities. Some men could not articulate possible reasons but others seemed to see the problems more clearly. Steve's [10] observation about the sexualization of coffee is an important example. Russell found the same problem in his study where close relationships with neighbourhood mothers was seen as a threat to marital relationships (1987, p. 172). Miriam Johnson (1988) points out that all cross-gender interaction in our society is sexualized on the dominant husband, subordinate wife model. This makes it difficult for men to participate in women's activities (such as coffee after the playgroup) as equals. It is also possible that because they are not doing gender in the expected ways, neighbourhood women are unsure of how to interact with them.

Carol's [14] assessment of her sister's reaction is also worth considering. Carol felt that she was resentful of the role reversal because it meant that a man could do what she (a stay-at-home mum) did. Women taking on a role which is less socially valued may resort to essentialist arguments to justify the importance of mothering and their allocation to that role. The fact that men *could* do it raises the possibility that they too had a choice. Or, it could be that women who have few real choices about employment (given current inequalities in that sphere) see such active fathers as encroaching on their only sphere of power, however limited that power is in reality (Lewis and O'Brien, 1987b, p. 15; Russell, 1987, p. 170).

There is also the question of the consequences for men of rejecting the societal model of masculinity or what Brannen and Moss refer to as the ideology of the 'good' father (1988, p. 16).

> Central to the ideology of male parenting is the belief that the father *should* be the main breadwinner, and that breadwinning is the most important role for the father.
>
> (Moss and Brannen, 1987, p. 41)

In my study, paid non-domestic work is not the primary role for the men in either role-reversal or shared-role arrangements nor does it form the major part of their identity.

Are there sanctions against men for refusing masculinity? Only Dave (21) speaks about his relationships with other men so it is difficult to tell but his difficulty forming male friendships poses some interesting questions. It is perhaps safe to assume that at least some men will react similarly to Dave's father, labelling men who mother as 'wimps' or 'poofs' and holding them accountable as *men* for their behaviour. Evidence from Russell's study lends some support to this view. Although most couples in his study reported initially positive reactions, continuing support was not in evidence.

> Only 35 percent of parents reported their relatives were consistently positive, 53 percent of fathers reported their male friends were negative, and 37 percent said their male workmates were negative.
>
> (Russell, 1987, p. 171)

He also found that female friends, relatives and colleagues reacted more positively. Similar evidence is found in Scott Coltrane's study of shared parenting (1989, pp. 485–8).

Some of the men in my study were able to develop networks of support. Steve [10] did not feel isolated in his community. Dave [21] had found the support of other men taking on similar roles, although he was disappointed with their level of commitment. Roger [15] had close friends in similar living arrangements. Roy [16] was involved in an anti-sexist men's network. However, the difficulties they face highlight the constraints facing most men.

Mothering without Men

Given these potential difficulties, it may be easier to transform mothering by not involving men. Maggie [2] says that not being in a relationship with a man is the best situation for her. Kate [1] talks about the benefits for her children of not concentrating on a couple relationship and notes that although she sometimes misses adult company this is more in terms of friendship than a couple relationship. Jane [4] stresses that mothering in a couple was never an issue for her even as a child. Ann [3] 'gradually became lesbian over the last 10 years or so' and stresses the importance of not looking for a man but working things out with women. Miriam [20] stresses the importance of her residential group being women only.

Despite their choice to 'mother without men', some of these women have relationships with men. Without diminishing the choices and struggles of lesbians living in a heterosexist and homophobic society, it is interesting to examine the way that sexuality and emotional relationships have been separated from housework and mothering for some of these women. The Parsonian nuclear family household not only incorporates a division of labour, it also presumes that all primary emotional relationships take place within it (thus enabling occupational mobility). Some of these women are disentangling them in a way that resembles what Marilyn Frye (1992) calls 'Virginity', a central aspect of radical feminist practice.[24] These women are trying to have sexual and emotional relationships (lesbian or heterosexual) while maintaining their independence from men.[25]

Given the structure of our society, refusing primary relationships with men is difficult. It is interesting that in the interview Jane [4] tries to justify the exclusion of the biological father of her child and comments that had the man with whom she had had a long-term relationship been the father, he might have had a role. This despite the fact that she also speaks of never, as a child, wanting to get married and wanting children only as a single parent. I interpret this as a (perhaps subconscious) response to social pressure to affirm the importance of fathers.

The social unacceptability of the rejection of men is perhaps also at the root of the problem of affirming the deliberate choice of single-mother status. Support is given on condition of accepting the evaluation that men *per se* are not the problem, it was just an individual man who abandoned the woman. Issues raised by lesbian feminists are perhaps relevant to the analysis of single mothers by choice. Women are held accountable as *women* for the ways that they choose to mother.

Notes

1　See Chapter 1, p. 13, for an explanation of my use of this term.
2　The importance of non-domestic work to identity will be discussed further in Chapter 5.
3　The samples often included the criterion 'at least one child under 5 years of age' (e.g. Oakley, 1974a).
4　For a summary of the feminist literature see Snitow (1992), Rowbotham (1989b) and Chapter 6 of Richardson (1993).
5　For a critical review of this literature see Delphy (1992).
6　Numbers in the text and tables refer to the descriptions of participants in Appendix 1.
7　For a critique of this approach see Thorne (1987).
8　My findings accord with those of the limited studies in this field. See Richardson (1993, pp. 125–43) for a review.
9　June Statham's (1986) book provides an example of this. Although she is studying non-sexist child-rearing, she includes a lot of information on relations between adults owing to the importance of providing role models. See also Coltrane (1989).
10　The essays in Dowrick and Grundberg's *Why Children?* (1980) provide an insight into this questioning.
11　Marilyn Frye has suggested a racist component of this pressure — preserving the 'white race' (1983b, esp. pp. 123–4).
12　Jane was using a combination of the rhythm method (she had a very predictable cycle) and diaphragm.
13　Although he knew she had come off the pill, he had never discussed contraception or offered to use condoms so she felt that he was leaving the choice (and the responsibility) to her. She has since confirmed with him that this was indeed his view.
14　Her relationship with her long-term partner continued for three years. The other relationship lasted three months. There was a period when she was openly in sexual relationships with two men.
15　See Morgan (1992, pp. 75–80) for a review of the literature linking masculine identity and work (narrowly defined).
16　See Chapter 3, Table 3.1 for details of child-care arrangements.

17 For a review of the relationship of motherhood, femininity and marriage and its effects on the public perception of single motherhood see Richardson (1993, pp. 76–7).

18 It is not possible to evaluate to what extent this is due to the fact that they are not using paid child-care. The children are still being looked after by one of their parents.

19 Paula is a member of the Working Mothers' Association, a national organization, but she is not happy with the title of 'working mothers' and neither are others in the local area. In 1994 the national organization changed its name to Parents at Work.

20 This pattern was also found by Coltrane (1989, pp. 485–8).

21 Hilary Graham (1982) argues that 'coping' is central to the definition and regulation of motherhood.

22 See Russell (1987) for a review of the limited literature on role reversals including his own study. The implicit definition of a role reversal used by Russell is men taking on child-care and women being main earners: 'reversing employment and child-care jobs, does not necessarily lead to fathers assuming the overall responsibility for children in the way that traditional mothers do. Many mothers retained greater responsibility for decision-making, planning, monitoring and anticipating the needs of the children, and "took over" when they arrived home from work' (1987, pp. 163–4). He also notes that women experienced difficulties similar to women in dual-earner couples related to *their dual roles*.

23 Indeed although the authors point out that other studies have shown that husbands and grandmothers are the most common relatives mentioned as looking after children, their data only show that 'a relative looks after them' (Witherspoon and Prior, 1991, p. 139) thus masking the extent of men's involvement.

24 She uses the term in its original meaning 'a female who is sexually and hence socially her own person'.

25 Although the material throws up interesting questions about sexuality, sexual practice and feminism, I do not have enough information to follow it up at this time.

Chapter 5

Non-domestic Work

In the course of discussing changes to the organization of their domestic lives, participants raised the topic of non-domestic work. Often this was paid work but some participants blurred the distinction between paid and unpaid non-domestic work. For others, non-domestic work, though important, was not currently bringing in any money. Whether paid or not, the organization and personal importance of non-domestic work was a major influence on anti-sexist living arrangements.

The discussion of the balance between mothering and non-domestic work was usually linked to the flexibility of paid non-domestic work. In contrast with government and business discourses of a flexible labour force, my respondents saw flexibility serving *their* needs and linked it to the need for adequate pay and conditions. Although, for some, flexibility was linked to a political critique of the current organization of non-domestic work in society, the overwhelming reason for seeking flexible non-domestic work was the desire to accommodate the needs of children. One should not assume, however, that the two are unrelated.

Another aspect of non-domestic work discussed in the interviews was identity. If mothering is not the only source of women's satisfaction, then something else must be important to their identities as well. This is often non-domestic work, usually paid. In some cases, the *specific* job is linked to their identity as feminists. Thus it is not merely having employment but the content of that employment which is important. For men, the fact of choosing to mother means having an identity less rooted in paid non-domestic work than might be expected. Societal expectations of men are linked to full-time paid work (Russell, 1987, p. 167).[1] Thus where women are trying to find an identity outside motherhood, men might be looking to both domestic and unpaid, non-domestic work.

Although the value that society places on paid productive work is important, the problem identified by early feminists (e.g. Friedan, 1963) was one of isolation and low self-esteem brought about by the focus of women's lives on the needs of others. From this point of view any activity which is focused on her own needs might be important for a woman's sense of identity. In my study paid work was not the only option. Many people are involved in political activism, further education, voluntary work, artistic pursuits and other social and leisure activities.

Some participants did not talk about non-domestic work in this way but rather as a way to bring in money. Flexible work was often talked about in relation to the ideas of affording alternatives and settling for less. Money also plays an important positive role in the resistance to and rejection of the role/ identity of wife. The allocation of financial resources within the living arrangement and the importance of financial independence for women will be discussed in the next chapter.

Non-domestic Work in Feminist Research

Feminist interest in work has in many ways mirrored the concerns of analyses of mothering. Where the latter tried to show that motherhood was not women's only source of happiness, the former focused on women's right to participate in paid work. Feminist interventions were also crucial in' problematizing the definition of work to include the domestic work of women — housework and mothering. But feminists quickly moved on from documenting the right of women to work, women's experience of work, and debunking the stereotypes of women and work (Beechey, 1987, Introduction).

The implication of the early analyses of women's isolation within the home was that employment held the key to women's emancipation, a view criticized by Black and working-class women for its failure to recognize the nature of the paid work many women did (e.g. hooks, 1984). These criticisms have led to analyses of labour markets and labour processes which attempt to explain the position of women in employment. A key issue in these analyses is the nature of the relationship between employment and domestic responsibilities. Is women's position in the labour market a result of their domestic responsibilities? Or is the responsibility of women for domestic work a result of their position in the labour market (Beechey, 1987)? More recent analyses have broadened the focus to take into account not only the links between the labour market and other institutions (primarily the family) but also the fact that the labour market is itself gendered (e.g. Acker, 1990; Beechey, 1988).

Carole Pateman's (1988) theoretical discussion of contract theory expands on this point. She notes that contractual relations between 'individuals' are based on a construction of the individual which is masculine. Joan Acker's (1990) theorization of organizations is similar. She points out that most organizational studies treat organizations and the rules that govern them as gender neutral. In particular, the notion of 'the job' which is to be filled by 'a worker' is disembodied. There is no way that the organization can take the bodily needs of the worker into account. These are assumed to be dealt with in the private sphere by someone else. Acker argues that this seemingly gender-neutral 'job' and the seemingly gender-neutral 'worker' that fills it, are in fact masculine and the 'someone else' is a wife. In Carole Pateman's terms the social contract includes a sexual contract.

This theoretical formulation could leave us with the impression that, to the extent that women can conform to this abstract ideal, they will have no problems with employment, thus focusing our attention back on the relationship between home and work, private and public. Pateman warns against this:

> Women are subject to men in both the private and public spheres; indeed, men's patriarchal right is the major structural support binding the two spheres into a social whole. Men's right of access to women's bodies is exercised in the public market as well as in private marriage, and patriarchal right is exercised over women and their bodies in ways other than direct sexual access.
>
> (Pateman, 1988, p. 113)

The main limitation of the literature in relation to my study is that it focuses primarily on employment. Very little attention has been paid to other forms of non-domestic work (with the notable exception of R. E. Pahl, 1984). Although this is understandable in the context of a society in which employment is the primary means of financial support and self-sufficiency is not feasible, it limits our understanding of the importance of other forms of work in the lives of men, women and children.[2] From the point of view of political transformation this is an important lack.

Because my study focuses on the home, I do not evaluate the patriarchal nature of the public sphere or the attempts to change that.[3] It will appear, in many cases, as a constraint on change in the private sphere. However, transforming the social relations of the private sphere requires the transformation of both the relationship between the public and the private, and the social relations of the public sphere. The discussion of non-domestic work is important as it indicates what those transformations might look like.

The class and race composition of the sample is particularly salient in this discussion. Most of those I interviewed had jobs that they enjoyed and saw non-domestic work as something which should be satisfying. Most also had well-paid jobs in sectors of the economy which may have been more influenced by arguments for equal opportunities than others (e.g. social work, teaching). Nevertheless, their experiences are instructive in that, even with this privileged position, most were constrained in some way by their employment. Clearly very few members of society have the options that these people do.

For the single mothers by choice flexibility and money were the most important issues. They discussed the importance of non-domestic work to their identities only in the context of the balance between non-domestic work and mothering (see Chapter 4). The relationship between non-domestic work and money was affected by the need of some of these women to pay for child-care. For the voluntarily childless heterosexual couples the important theme was money, particularly in relation to women's independence. For women in this category the relationship between non-domestic work and identity was clearly linked to specific jobs. All three themes were important for both categories of heterosexual couples with children. The primary difference here was the way flexibility, as a lived reality, affected their living arrangements. The actual non-domestic work situations of the people in these two categories affected the discussion of non-domestic work in relation to identity. Although a more diverse category, the multiple adult arrangements were the only category in which the importance of flexibility was not related to the existence of children. Flexibility was the important theme here. Arrangements that resembled those in other categories often had similar important themes and will be compared.

Flexibility

For those whose identities are linked to multiple roles, flexibility in paid work is extremely important and is one topic which differentiates one group of respondents from the rest. The form of flexibility is often one which questions the logic of the 'abstract job' filled by the 'abstract worker' as specified by Acker (1990). Flexible non-domestic work arrangements were considerably more important for those with children than for those without children. They were also a key factor in the decision of heterosexual couples with children to adopt one living arrangement instead of another.

Single Mothers by Choice

The 'abstract worker' described by Acker has a partner (a wife). Single people can only be workers to the extent that their personal needs are not so great that they interfere with the job. Flexibility is thus of prime importance for single mothers.

Maggie [2][4] found her former job as a social worker too demanding and inflexible at short notice and now teaches social work at a local college. She is working full time but says that she might prefer to work part time if she could afford it. Kate [1] has also changed jobs for more flexibility although in her case it has put her in a 'financially precarious' situation. She has pursued several career options in the past 20 years: an MA in the city where her mother lived; one year teaching part time but mainly home with her daughter; a Certificate in Education; and teaching both full and part time for several years. Kate is now a freelance scriptwriter but has returned to teaching when necessary. Some of her teaching jobs were more flexible than others but she notes that employers' needs (i.e. a teacher shortage) had more influence on flexibility than any other factor. Ann [3] was able to do half-time building work in the commune were she lived when her children were young. Since leaving the commune, she has taught part time in adult education but was not able to make a career of that and now works as a part-time administrator for two housing co-operatives.

Jane [4] has not been able to find suitable paid non-domestic work and has found that the 'abstract worker' model is supported by the state. Benefit regulations regarding the treatment of earnings do not take account of her mothering role. Nevertheless, Jane had taken the first part of an Open University course and had had two very low-paid, very part-time jobs where Dorothy could come with her. She also writes for a magazine (which pays little and infrequently) and has a long-term writing project (unpaid) in progress. She has supplemented her income with prostitution on occasion.

Although important, the availability of flexible non-domestic work is not sufficient for single mothers by choice. Many women's ability to engage in non-domestic work is related to the availability of practical support for which they do not have to pay. Their paid work must pay well enough not only to support the living arrangement but also, in some cases, to pay for child-care. It is interesting to note the type of non-domestic paid work these women have taken: teaching, writing, and work in politically aware organizations (commune, housing co-ops).

Jo VanEvery

Heterosexual Couples with Children with Shared Roles

Like the single mothers by choice, those in this category seek flexible non-domestic work situations in order to fit in with their commitment to looking after their children themselves and so that the child-care and housework are divided equally. Rejecting the role/identity of wife entails rejecting the role/identity of worker. Only one couple in this group used full-time paid child-care and they are unsatisfied with the fit between their non-domestic work and home lives. It is interesting to compare the couples in this category with those in role-reversal situations as some of the latter might have chosen this option if the necessary flexibility were available.

Jean and Eric [18] work from home and do not distinguish between paid and voluntary work when they discuss their 'work'. Jean does freelance work for several organizations, for many of which she also does voluntary work, and has a part-time job as a development officer for the local child-minding association. Eric was working as a part-time secretary for a local organization but now does freelance secretarial work and sets up computer systems for voluntary organizations and small businesses. He also does voluntary work, often for the same organizations as Jean.

Roy and Alice [16] also blur the boundaries somewhat between voluntary work, political activism and paid work. Although it is only since the children are older that Alice has taken full-time paid work, she was combining motherhood with voluntary work and a term as a local councillor when her two youngest were babies. She has also worked in both teaching and social work. Alice is currently coordinating a community mental health programme, a job which has some flexibility, partly because of her senior position. Roy is a teacher and has always worked part time although the number of days has changed. He is also actively involved in politics.

Carolyn and Roger [15] have had some difficulty arranging their paid work to their satisfaction. Their best experience was a job-share in a university overseas but it was difficult to organize and not well thought out. For example, there was no provision for maternity leave. It was assumed that one would take over for the other in that situation. Recently Carolyn has been appointed to a part-time teaching position at a local university and Roger will fit his part-time Teaching English as a Foreign Language work around it. Although other participants have found teaching quite flexible, their experience of part-time employment (particularly in universities) is of low pay and exploitative conditions with little support from the unions.

Paula and Rob [17] have had similar problems. They work full time in social services and have had jobs in the public and voluntary sectors. They have changed jobs several times in the search for flexible non-domestic work

94

closer to where they live. Paula has had a lot of difficulty finding suitable work: the most flexible was too far away; part time was unsatisfactory; and her current full-time position is inflexible. She still doesn't know what the ideal is (full time or part time) and they have talked about whether it would be better if Rob worked part time or gave up paid work.

Although flexibility is important to the people in this category in order to achieve their ideal living arrangement, many have experienced problems in finding suitable employment. Availability of child-care is not as important as it is for single mothers but is in some ways more directly related to the availability of flexible non-domestic (especially paid) work. One partner's flexible non-domestic work is the other partner's child-care.

Heterosexual Couples with Children in Role-reversal Situations

As we have seen, especially in the case of housework, the role reversals are rejecting and resisting the role/identity of wife in a very different way from the other participants. The nature of this difference is clear when we examine the flexibility of their non-domestic work. Unlike those with shared roles, they have not rejected the role/identity of worker. However, most of the people in this group spoke of maybe arranging their lives differently if the opportunities had been there.

Paid work is often inflexible for people in this category. Rebecca [12] mentions that she is the first woman working in her local library system to return to work after maternity leave and that she has a friend who had wanted to return part time and was refused. Similarly, Christiane [11] explored the possibility of doing half a job for the firm of accountants who employ her but they said it was impossible. Owing to his senior position and his ability to convince his superiors that he wouldn't start a trend, Wilhelm was able to get a 16-month leave of absence but is doubtful of his ability to change the long hours usually required in his job. Linda [13] also remarks on the inflexibility of her employer, a trade union.

For others in this category flexibility is not such an important issue. Because Steve [10] was not attached to paid work, Liz never had to worry about the flexibility of her job. She mentions that had he wanted to work outside the home they would have sorted something out but it was clearly never an important issue. Similarly, Patrick's [14] offer to be the primary carer obviated the need for Carol to consider the flexibility of her non-domestic work. In her case, however, if the offer had not been made, she wouldn't have had children.

Until Dan [13] offered to take the children full time, Linda was aware that her non-domestic work was inflexible but had never considered anything but muddling through. In the past she had given up paid work in her field and worked as a child-minder, which she disliked, because it fitted in with her child-care responsibilities. Part of her enjoyment of the current arrangement is related to the relief of some of the stress of trying to be a worker and a mother.

It is interesting to compare the types of paid work that the people in this category did with that done by those in the shared roles category. Liz [10] is a social worker; Rebecca [12] a librarian; Christiane [11] an accountant; Wilhelm [11] a business executive; Linda [13] a secretary; and Carol [14] runs her own business. Liz and Carol could possibly arrange more flexible paid work but Carol doesn't want to and Liz doesn't need to.[5] For the others, the attitudes and practices of their employers were central. In contrast those with shared roles worked primarily as teachers or in social services. Nevertheless, it was obvious that even in these areas there was considerable variation, as evidenced by the problems Paula and Rob [17], and Carolyn and Roger [15] were experiencing.

Other Arrangements with Children

The situation of a lesbian couple, Kathryn and Amy [28], highlights the constraints imposed on living arrangements by the employment available. Between the births of their two children Amy and Kathryn both worked two and a half days a week. It was not easy to arrange (Kathryn had to threaten to take her employer, a trade union, to a tribunal) but they found it satisfactory. When Amy became pregnant, Kathryn switched back to full-time employment but felt that, although they would prefer their earlier arrangement, it would be too problematic to switch back again at the end of Amy's maternity leave.

Kathryn then took a job abroad where Amy couldn't work because of immigration regulations. When they returned Amy started looking for full-time employment and Kathryn planned to stay home because they have a commitment to maintaining their earning power at relatively equal levels and to allowing each to spend time with the children. Amy spent a period of time doing temporary office jobs during which she observed the difficulty of arranging flexible work in a business environment. Kathryn took a part-time job, which she still has, partly because of the difficulty Amy was having and partly to maintain her earning power. Amy found a job in the voluntary sector and, although she had to start at a low salary owing to the period of full-time mothering, she has since had promotions.

The constraints imposed by employers are clearly visible in Amy and Kathryn's case. Not only did they have to threaten an industrial tribunal at one stage but they also encountered a lack of understanding of time out of paid employment for mothering. Like other couples with children they are dependent on each other for most of the support necessary to combine mothering and non-domestic work. The difference between their situation and that of the heterosexual role reversals is that they have decided to share roles over time, switching between paid work and mothering so that both have equal involvement in both spheres. The theoretical formulation which I have used would lead me to the conclusion that this option was open to them (as two women) in a way that it was not for heterosexual couples. Although they are not free from doing gender, the relationship (of dominance and subordination) between men and women is not enacted on an ongoing basis within their home (cf. Berk, 1985, pp. 203–4).

Multiple Adult Arrangements

In this category flexible non-domestic work patterns were not as closely linked to child-care arrangements as for the other categories. There was a rejection of and resistance to the role/identity of worker even where the extra personal responsibilities of motherhood were absent.

In the Peterson household [22], Val worked full time as a civil servant and Jason worked freelance from home. Their situation is similar to that of Roy and Alice [16] (and their children are about the same ages) but the arrangement has evolved much more recently. The strains of being a worker were brought home to Jason when he suffered a breakdown. Previously Val did voluntary work, helped at the school, was a local councillor and a school governor. She started doing paid non-domestic work slowly, working one day a week and then doing flexible research jobs that allowed her to work from home. As Jason needed to reduce his workload, Val wanted to increase hers. Her current job is relatively inflexible.

Miriam [20] teaches in further education and values the autonomy part-time work on short-term contracts gives her although the pay and conditions are worse than if she took a permanent post in a similar institution. Like the other single mothers by choice, she is heavily dependent on having enough money coming in as well as child-care support. Her living arrangement thus has the advantage of lowering the costs and providing some informal child-care.

Lynne and Dave [21] differ slightly from the other role reversals because Lynne's job as a researcher is relatively flexible and she often works from home. Dave does freelance building work and could work more than he does if he wished. The flexibility of his paid work has allowed him to spend a lot of time with the children in the past but now allows him to pursue other non-domestic work particularly artistic expression through pottery.

The other two arrangements in this group are collective households. The urban collective [19] has members both in and out of paid work. Some are doing artistic work which is currently unpaid. Laura works as a freelance accountant from home. Chris is a full-time researcher at the local university. Beth works full time in the insurance industry and part time in a pub. Flexibility in this living arrangement is related to work satisfaction and the importance of unpaid non-domestic work activities.

There are children in the rural collective [23] but some of the members have been there since before the children arrived and their interest in flexible work patterns is also not related to children. They are involved in the New Age movement. Sara works part time for the local authority and spends a lot of her time working in the garden at home. Alex is a therapist and, because of the difficulties involved in setting up an independent practice, he works away from home more often than he would like. Mary used to work as a teacher but the last time she was in full-time paid work she ended up with a serious stress-related illness and decided that she would rather live on state benefits, spend time with her children and be healthy. Eleanor does voluntary work with various organizations and collects a pension. The lower individual costs of living in this sort of arrangement and the fact that the rural collective grow some of their own food and fuel make these flexible work-styles more possible.

Again flexibility is found in jobs which may be done on a freelance basis, research jobs and local authority employment. Those not in paid work are often engaged in other forms of non-domestic work. The existence of other adults in the living arrangement diminishes the reliance on one other adult or paid external support for child-care or financial maintenance.

Voluntarily Childless

The link between voluntary childlessness and non-domestic work was not strong in my study. Most of the respondents didn't mention flexibility as an issue although they recognized the problems inflexibility might have posed had they had children. Without the increased responsibilities of motherhood it was possible to reject and resist the role/identity of wife without challenging the construction of the role/identity of worker.

In contrast with the childless members of collectives, who were often critical of the organization of non-domestic work, only two women (Pat [24] and Karen [6]) sought flexible paid work in order to support their more satisfying non-domestic pursuits. Unlike those in collectives, they didn't have the option of collecting state benefits either because of presumed dependency on a husband (Karen) or owing to the inadequacy of those benefits to meet expenses (greater when living alone than in a collective). Interestingly both Karen and Pat consider themselves to be writers although they make no money from their writing. Pat has taken a part-time clerical job and Karen is training as a counsellor in order to bring in money.[6] Pat also does some guest lectures at universities and is critical of the organization and pay of guest lecturing which assumes that the lecturer has a full-time academic job. Others in this category took a very conventional attitude to non-domestic work fitting political, voluntary and other non-domestic interests around full-time paid work.

The availability of flexible non-domestic work clearly influences the form of anti-sexist living arrangements. The role/identity of wife, identified as central to women's oppression, has its complement in the role/identity of worker. By rejecting one, the construction of the other may be brought into question. This is especially the case in living arrangements with children. It is clear that many women (and men) lack control over their non-domestic work choices. It is also clear that some jobs seem to be more flexible than others. For those whose employers are politically aware and committed to equality, the situation is easier. Others have taken the option of freelance paid work although this is often financially unpredictable.

Identity

Structural locations in a system are accompanied by forms of self-identity. The theoretical framework which informs my work shows how hegemonic constructions of identity have a single primary component with other areas as strictly secondary. Thus the paid work that wives do is not central to their identity but that of husbands is. Balance is created through the complementarity of roles/identities within a residential group (i.e. one worker and one wife). I have suggested that rejecting the role/identity of wife can lead to the rejection of the role/identity of worker. How does non-domestic work relate to identity in this situation? I will look at the relationship of non-domestic work to identity for both women and men and also talk about the conditions in which respondents seemed to take non-domestic work for granted.

The importance of non-domestic work to the identities of the single mothers was usually expressed in terms of striking the right balance between non-domestic work and mothering. Despite a variety of employment patterns, none would be satisfied with either full-time mothering or full-time employment, indicating the possibility of constructing an identity with several equally important elements. The difficulties they have experienced with practical and political support and flexibility indicate the radical nature of such an identity.

Heterosexual Couples with Reversed Roles

One might consider that the relationship between non-domestic work and identity for those in role-reversal situations would be similar to traditional identities with the genders reversed. Thus perhaps women would get their identity from their non-domestic work, and men from their mothering. The situation is not that clear. I will consider the men and the women separately.[7]

In Christiane's [11] case we can see the move from an acceptance of the identity of wife/mother, to its rejection in favour of that of worker, to a desire for an identity which balances both.[8] This has been frustrated by the inflexibility of her non-domestic work. Liz [10] has been luckier and practical constraints have not prevented her from translating her eagerness to use her qualifications and her enthusiasm for education into practice. Although she is now tired of her job and frustrated with the internal politics, she still wants to work and is looking for employment in a related field perhaps teaching on a social work course, indicating the importance of non-domestic work to her identity. Lynne's [21] eagerness to take her university degree is similar to Liz's in many respects. Lynne and Dave identify the particular strength of their living arrangement as Lynne's identity as her own person and not *just* as Dave's 'other half' or the children's mother.

Linda [13] told me that she was surprised at how she felt about the change to a role reversal encompassing two residential groups. Previously, being a mother had been quite important to her identity but now she has realized that it is not as important as she thought. The change has also allowed her to train for a different kind of job, a prospect which she finds quite liberating. She does not express this as changing to the other option (from wife to worker) but as somehow combining non-domestic work and mothering.

Men in role reversals seem to be completely unattached to paid work as a source of identity. In contrast with Liz's [10] eagerness, Steve was not that attached to non-domestic work. He may take a part-time job now that the children are both in school but that would only be for the money. Similarly,

Patrick [14] is uninterested in paid work although he was considered a high flyer in a management training programme for a large company before the children were born.

Dave's [21] initial decision was motivated by the needs of their children, and while the children were younger his interests revolved primarily around them, although he did take some courses and got involved in some political activism. However, there is evidence that he has rejected both conventional identities, including the decision to stop mothering the two younger foster children. In addition, he was disappointed with other men involved in the Fathers' Network who reverted to conventional roles when their children were older. Dave is now spending a lot of time doing pottery. He has continued to do some construction and mechanical work on a freelance basis since leaving formal employment but the amount is dictated primarily by his own desire to do this kind of work and to get out of the house.

Despite the low attachment to paid work of these three men, their withdrawal from paid employment was related to taking on child-care responsibilities. In contrast, the link between non-domestic work and Jack's [12] identity is the type of work. Jack had already stopped working full time to try to make a living writing songs before he and Rebecca made the decision to have a child. He plays in a band and is now working with an artist friend writing children's books. Owing to financial pressures he also works part time in a supermarket. His identity can be seen to be combining two important elements. Similarly, Dan and Linda [13] changed their arrangements because Dan wanted to devote more of his time to political activism.

Wilhelm's [11] situation has aspects of both motivations. Although his withdrawal from work was precipitated by child-care responsibilities, he had always been critical of the conventional worker identity and planned to take some time out. Wilhelm sees the arrival of children as the 'perfect excuse'. Like Christiane, the inflexibility of his non-domestic work limits his ability to translate this radical identity into practice.

Heterosexual Couples with Shared Roles

Like the single mothers, the importance of non-domestic work to identity for heterosexual couples with shared roles is primarily about the balance between non-domestic work and mothering. None of the men in this category is as unattached to paid work as those in the role-reversal situations but they are critical of the masculine norm of full-time employment. For some, paid work was seen primarily as a way to bring in money, a topic that will be discussed further below.

Eric's [18] relationship to non-domestic work is similar to that of the men in role-reversal situations. Although he is currently working freelance doing full-time hours he frequently raised the issue of their initial agreement to reverse roles. However, given that both he and Jean are involved in both paid and voluntary work (often for the same organizations) and make little distinction between the two, it is hard to imagine that Eric's identity would have been totally related to his mothering role. Rob [17] says that he is lucky to have work that he enjoys and that it is more of a hobby than an obligation. In contrast, Roger [15] would like to retrain but has neither the time nor the money to do so. His particular job is not important to his identity although the desire to retrain indicates that some non-domestic work might be.

Roy [16] expresses his identity in terms of a triangle of work, politics and family. All three are equally important and he tries to balance them. This orientation is closest to that of the women in the study. It involves a critique of the traditional separation of non-domestic work from other things and an attempt to reach a better balance. The subjects that Roy teaches and the teaching methods used are heavily influenced by his political beliefs: he was involved in the introduction of an anti-sexist life skills course in a boys' school and in a move to have cooking facilities in all boys' schools in his area.

Both Jean [18] and Alice [16] have been relatively successful in constructing a balanced identity. Jean had refused to marry a previous partner because he expected her to stop working when she had children. She also opted for freelance work over a full-time job in a community centre because she found it more satisfying. Alice has been involved in paid, voluntary and political work and, like Jean, all types are interlinked. Despite the guilt at leaving her children, her work is important to her identity, and she will probably work full time until retirement. Neither Carolyn [15] nor Paula [17] were happy with full-time mothering. However, their attempts to construct a more balanced identity have been constrained by their employment options.

Voluntarily Childless

The link between non-domestic work and identity was not as strongly expressed by the voluntarily childless. Perhaps the balancing of non-domestic work and mothering leads to an articulation of the importance of non-domestic work that otherwise might not occur. The men in this category hardly talked about non-domestic work at all except to tell me what their job was. The way they treated the question in the interview indicated the taken-for-granted character of conventional identities. This was also true for some of the women. Roseanne [5] is an example of this type.

Roseanne is a civil servant and had recently had a promotion but was not sure what she would *like* to do in terms of paid work. Although she didn't express dislike of her work, neither did she express any enthusiasm for it. Roseanne's identity is clearly *not* linked to domestic work and seemed to be more focused on her leisure interests of reading and cinema. She had also been taking an Open University course which related to these interests and had been politically active.

Other voluntarily childless women had identities much more tied to non-domestic work. This was not to non-domestic work in general but to the specific type of non-domestic work they did. Karen [6] is one example. Her identity as a writer clearly influences other decisions about her life — the importance of flexible paid work, (partly) her decision to remain childless, and the amount of domestic work she does. She explicitly compares the importance of writing in her life to the importance of Pete's job in his.

Peg's [7] identity *as a feminist* seems to be linked with her non-domestic work. She stresses the importance of the fact that she works almost exclusively with women (both colleagues and clients) in her job as a health visitor. Part of her job is to provide a health visiting service to the local Women's Aid refuge. Her commitment to women and to feminism also influences her work with Women's Aid. Louise [8] is also a nurse now working with an agency, mostly with the elderly. She used to work in public hospitals and she is critical of the status of nurses in that sector, and the way that the gender hierarchy affects the work environment. In contrast, she finds the situation of nurses in homes for the elderly, where there are few doctors and mostly women staff, much more supportive. Louise would like to get into community nursing but has decided not to pursue the necessary training in preference for developing her interest in alternative therapies.

Both Pat [24] and Lisa [25] said that they had never imagined not working even when married and Lisa mentioned giving up non-domestic work as a deterrent to having children. Pat radically changed career a few years ago. She experienced a period of adjustment between the two. Pat had been attached to both types of career although they had very different work patterns: the first working long hours in the publishing industry (the conventional worker model); the second working part time for money and concentrating on writing. Lisa [25] is a teacher in an all-girls' school and, like Louise [8] and Peg [7], enjoys working in an environment that is predominantly women. She also integrates feminist ideas into her teaching trying to get her students to question images of women that they encounter and introducing them to a variety of possibilities.

Many of those in both the urban [19] and rural [23] collectives had unconventional attitudes to non-domestic work. In the rural collective, non-domestic work was linked to political beliefs (e.g. Sara's work involved the provision of education for Travellers). Mary had clearly rejected the conventional worker model (because of its effect on her health) and was constrained from pursuing a better balance. Most of those in the urban collective [19] were doing unpaid artistic work. Laura was working freelance as an accountant and also pursuing some unpaid interests. Chris expressed a willingness to change his work pattern indicative of an identity similar to other men in the study. Beth was the only one with a fairly conventional attitude to non-domestic work, pursuing advancement in a career she did not like much and working part time in another job as well.

Miriam's [20] rejection of the conventional identity of worker is indicated by her preference for short-term contracts with several institutions over a better paid, permanent job. There is evidence too that the type of work is also important. She had done some work with social services aimed at getting young people back into education.

The importance of non-domestic work to Jason's [22] identity is unclear. In the interview he frequently confused 'work' with 'breadwinning'. His orientation to work did change after a breakdown and he talks frequently of the 'evolution' of new patterns within the living arrangement. Val expressed discontent with full-time mothering but still rates family as more important than her non-domestic work. She qualifies this, however, with the fact that she doesn't like her current job.

There is evidence in the interviews of a reconstruction of forms of personal identity which is linked to non-domestic work. This is most evident for those with children although this is limited in many cases by practical constraints. The only group for whom the role/identity of worker seems to have been taken up was the voluntarily childless men. Childless women modified this identity to the extent that they introduced political concerns into their identities as workers. Unlike the findings of other studies, women did not express a desire to be full-time mothers if possible, and men's identities were not threatened by the lack of full-time, paid non-domestic work.

Non-domestic Work and Money

So far I have documented the ways in which the rejection of and resistance to the role/identity of wife entails a reconstruction of its complement, the role/identity of worker. Money is an important factor in this type of political action. There are two issues to be considered in relation to money: affording alternatives and settling for less. In the interviews the two are intertwined usually through the construction of what is 'enough' money.

As Michèle Barrett and Mary McIntosh have pointed out:

> Those who have managed to choose and establish other ways of living have tended to be better off, or else willing to put up with considerable material privation.
>
> (1982, p. 148)

If flexible non-domestic work (part-time or freelance) doesn't earn enough to maintain the living arrangement (and, in some cases, pay for child-care) it won't be a possibility. The educational attainment and class background of the participants make them particularly likely to be able to afford these alternative living arrangements. The people who took part in my study were usually in relatively well-paid jobs and thus had the option of working less. This option is not open to most although the financial benefits of multiple adult arrangements may compensate in some cases.

Despite the importance of non-domestic work to identity for men and women, and the fact that many enjoyed their non-domestic work, many respondents said that non-domestic work was about getting money in. It is precisely the concept of 'enough money' that is the issue for them. They recognize the fact that if they organized their lives differently they would have more money but are unwilling to do so because of the importance of the principles behind that organization. This is most obvious for those with children. In addition, many did without certain things which are often taken for granted (e.g. new clothes, cars) in order to pursue their political goals. Again this can be seen as a constraint to the extent that it assumes there are areas in which one can cut back. For many people survival requires all their energy and limits their choices.

Single mothers by choice face particular problems in relation to earning enough money for the living arrangement. They form the bulk of the cases in this study whose aggregate incomes fall below the national median household income. Maggie [2] talks about perhaps wanting to work part time but not being able to afford it. This is at least partly due to a particular standard of living which she would like to maintain. In addition to her salary, she gets extra money from renting rooms in her house. In contrast, Jane [4] would like to work part time instead of claiming state benefits. However, because of the treatment of earnings by the Department of Social Security, the cost of child-care, and the possible loss of Housing Benefit, she cannot afford to do so. For Maggie [2] and Kate [1], being able to afford paid child-care is also crucial.

Although Ann [3] has not 'decided' to live on less money (she has never found a way of earning more), she feels that if she can manage on what she earns, she would prefer time for the children and other activities over more money. Kate [1] refers to her situation as 'financially precarious' but values the flexibility of working freelance from home over a more stable income.

I discussed the possible constraints imposed on heterosexual couples by gender inequalities in the labour market with Kathryn and Amy [28]. Their response was quite clear.

> I don't think you can make a serious attempt to live in an alternative way unless you say 'we're prepared to sacrifice that for the greater good of giving the kids a bit of access to their fathers'. I mean we were prepared to live on much less income in the interests of equality of access to the children.
>
> (Kathryn)

This is clearly the case for the heterosexual couples with children with shared roles who often talk about non-domestic work as necessary to finance the living arrangement. In the case of Paula and Rob [17], who are both working full time, it was a backwards career move for Rob to work locally and he took a cut in pay. They say that they are lucky to be able to afford a private nursery because state provision of child-care in their area is almost non-existent and they have no informal support. Jean and Eric [18] are also earning less by working freelance than if they had stayed with their original plan of Jean working full time. Roy and Alice [16] talk about their current joint income as a 'temporary high' and are using it for some of the things they have previously done without, like decorating.

Although Carolyn and Roger [15] recognize that they are living on less money than they could potentially earn, their inability to find suitable paid work dominates the interview. They lack the resources (both time and money) to enable either of them to retrain. Their division of non-domestic work is therefore seen in terms of allowing both to spend time with the children and bringing in 'enough' money. There are certain standards that they will not compromise, especially the kind of food they eat, but their needs are reduced by a low mortgage and not owning a car. However, Roger sometimes worries about longer term financial issues such as pensions.

For those in role reversals it is recognized that were both partners in full-time paid work they would have more money but they attach more importance to one of them being there most of the time. It is less common to say that money is the motivation for non-domestic work. Liz [10] does the work because she enjoys it and the fact that they can live on her income allows Steve to spend the time caring for the children and pursuing other interests. She alerts us to the constructed character of an 'adequate' standard of living:

> For my friend [Judy] at work this would be poverty. This would be poverty. You know really. . . . But for me it's quite comfortable.
>
> (Liz)

Although Liz has a middle-class occupation and high academic qualifications, the fact that she has a working-class background affects this perception. The situations of Carol [14] and Linda [13] are similar. Rebecca [12] does say that she works for the money (although she enjoys her paid work more since she has been promoted to a management position). She would rather work part time if Jack could get well-paid part-time work and her employer was that flexible, but recognizes that this is unlikely.

The advantage of multiple adult arrangements is that they are cheaper to live in than smaller residential groups. In the rural collective [23], this allows Mary some comfort on state benefits and also allows Sara to survive on part-time work. Mary's decision to claim state benefits instead of doing paid work didn't involve losing her independence as it would for women in heterosexual couples living on their own because she could still claim state benefits.

Miriam's [20] situation is similar to that of the single mothers by choice. Difficulties with the co-owner of her house have diminished this advantage. Her financial worries are focused on being able to afford the house on her own. This has meant working more than she would like to and taking an extra lodger. Despite the lower pay and conditions of part-time, sessional teaching and her current financial problems, Miriam was resisting giving up the flexibility. Since the interview she has taken a 'proper contract'.

Like the women in the role-reversal situations, Lynne [21] also feels that she works for enjoyment and her high income enables their living arrangement. However, she has felt the pressure of being a breadwinner more recently. She has lost her confidence in the possibility that Dave would go back to full-time paid work if necessary.

For the voluntarily childless money is usually not a problem. Not having children reduces expenses considerably. This had the knock-on effect of giving them more options regarding the division of domestic work (e.g. eating out regularly). In Karen's [6] case it also allowed her to pursue an unpaid career although the dependency that resulted was unsatisfactory. Pat [24], a voluntarily childless single woman, had chosen to settle for less money. She left a well-paid full-time job in publishing to pursue her writing.

Although she claimed state benefits for a while these were inadequate and she now supports herself with a part-time clerical job.

It is here that we can see a major factor constraining others from pursuing anti-sexist living arrangements and part of the explanation for the class bias of the sample. Many people are not in the position to settle for less and cannot afford alternatives even if they wanted to try them. Despite Kathryn's comment, the difference in men's and women's average wages and their positions in the labour market act as a considerable constraint on pursuing anti-sexist living arrangements.

Conclusions

In the two previous chapters I have dealt with roles/identities usually considered internal to the private sphere (i.e. wife, mother). However, as Carole Pateman emphasizes, the two spheres are intimately connected and both are gendered. The role/identity of wife has its complement in the role/identity of worker/breadwinner. Other studies have shown how these two roles/identities are maintained and enforced in the public sphere (e.g. Cockburn, 1991). I have looked outward from the homes of my participants to see how they affect the ability to transform families.

Women (especially as mothers) confront the same problems as women in conventional living arrangements — the difficulties of combining non-domestic work with domestic responsibilities. The men in my study also face these problems because they have taken on responsibilities usually delegated to wives. Joan Acker (1990) explains that the worker is constructed as someone who lives for the job and has no other pressing demands on his time.[9] The role/identity of worker is resisted and rejected through the demands for flexible work with decent pay and conditions, and the attempt to reconstruct identities which include multiple elements (non-domestic, domestic, caring relation-ships, etc.). The pattern is not as visible for the childless (whose domestic responsibilities are fewer) unless they have a commitment to non-economic values for which they make time (e.g. the rural collective, those who are writers). This resistance is limited by the structure of the labour market and by individuals' abilities to survive on the money they can earn in these ways.

There is also some evidence of influence in the other direction. The desire to transform families has an effect on people's participation in non-domestic work. In some cases this led to pressure on employers to introduce more flexibility. And economic rationality is subverted by a desire to earn 'enough' in the least amount of time rather than earn more and more working a standard week.

Notes

1   Supporting evidence is also found in Ann Oakley's study (1974b) in which most
    people thought it would be strange for a woman to go out to work and a man to take
    care of children; and in the studies of Brannen and Moss (1988, 1991) and
    Hochschild (1989) in which most respondents rated the husband's job as more
    important regardless of the relative income or occupational status of the wife's job.
2   There are almost no studies of children's work (see O'Brien, forthcoming).
3   See Cockburn (1991) who uses Pateman's work to understand the successes and
    failures of equal opportunities in Britain.
4   Numbers in the text and tables refer to the descriptions of participants in Appendix
    1.
5   However, other social workers in the study noted that, despite the flexible nature of
    the work, it was difficult to rearrange things at short notice.
6   The importance of financial independence to anti-sexist living arrangements will be
    discussed in the next chapter.
7   Although classified as a multiple adult arrangement, I will consider Lynne and Dave
    [21] with the role-reversal situations for this theme owing to their similarity.
8   See Chapter 4, p. 75.
9   The pronoun 'his' is intentional. As Acker points out this abstract worker is
    masculine.

Chapter 6

Financial Independence

Affording alternatives and settling for less were not the only money issues discussed in the interviews. The distribution of money within the household and the relative importance of who earned it were also discussed. Feminists have identified financial dependence as an important factor in women's oppression. In sociology, households and families are defined (at least partly) as units which redistribute resources both between adults and from adults to children. These resources include money, food and clothing as well as emotional and psychological support. Recent research (e.g. J. Pahl, 1983, 1989) has shown that this redistribution cannot be assumed to be equal and has highlighted the relationship between the distribution of financial resources and the distribution of power within households.[1]

Lydia Morris (1990) provides a detailed review and discussion of this literature in both the UK and the USA. The characteristic of this research that stands out from my perspective is the extent to which it focuses on the relationship between the labour market and the household and takes for granted particular constructions of gender. Thus, for example, Morris points out 'that implicit in the asking of the question "why work?" is the assumption that for married women at least some alternative means of support is available' (1990, p. 117). In addition, this body of research focuses almost exclusively on married couples (or fails to distinguish between married and cohabiting couples). Only one study includes lesbian and gay couples (Blumstein and Schwartz, 1983) and there is no discussion of other arrangements or household forms.

Research into the allocation of financial resources within households has been heavily influenced (in Britain) by the work of Jan Pahl, particularly her typology of systems of financial management. The four systems of management used in Pahl's classification are whole wage, allowance, joint management (or pooling), and independent management. The *whole wage* system is one in which the entire wage is given over to one partner (usually the wife) who then gives back some personal spending money and takes responsibility for paying all the bills.[2] The *allowance* system is one in which the primary earner gives over an allowance (commonly called housekeeping) which is meant to cover certain specified expenses. *Joint management* usually involves a joint bank account or (at lower income levels where wages are paid weekly in cash) a drawer or jar in which all money is kept. Both partners have access to all the money and take joint responsibility for paying the bills. *Independent management* may or may not involve a joint account or 'kitty' for bills but is distinguished by the fact that neither partner has access to all the money (each retains some independent money). In her more recent work (with Carolyn Vogler), Pahl has usefully distinguished between male and female managed variants of each type and has incorporated systems of control (see Vogler and Pahl, 1993, 1994).

The social relations which I have identified as being central to the nuclear family household are power relations. One way in which the complementarity of wife and worker is maintained is through the medium of money. The worker is a breadwinner with a wife who is maintained by him. If, as I argue, the defining characteristic of *anti-sexist* living arrangements is the rejection of and resistance to the role/identity of wife, there should also be evidence in the allocation of financial resources.

The Allocation of Financial Resources within Anti-sexist Living Arrangements

To facilitate the discussion of the allocation of money I have classified my sample using Pahl's (1989) classification of systems of money management. Pahl's work was limited to heterosexual couples with children but it easily extends to childless couples. The largest problem with using this classification for my study is that it was developed for living arrangements consisting of (married) couples and no other adults. Living arrangements which span more than one residential group are difficult to classify as are living arrangements with more than two adults, particularly when they do not revolve around a couple. I have classified those who live alone as having an independent management system. Although this seems almost meaningless, independence is an important reason that they live alone and may be important for purposes of explanation.[3]

Both the whole wage and the allowance systems were absent in my study. This is hardly surprising given that most research has shown that these two systems of money management are most commonly found in lower income groups. Although incomes in my study vary from Income Support to over £200000 per annum, the majority (20/25) of the respondents have an aggregate income[4] above the 1991 median household income of £297.47 per week (Central Statistical Office, 1992, p. 8). Those whose incomes were below the median are primarily single women although there is one couple (in the category of heterosexual couples with children with shared roles) and all use independent management systems.

The most striking finding of my research is the prevalence of the independent management system. Two-thirds of the participants used an independent management system of which four living arrangements used a partial pool for major bills and three more had a kitty for essentials and/or food. The other third used a joint management system. As Morris points out 'Being of low incidence this [independent management] is not a finance system which has received much research attention' (1989, p. 457). Income does not explain why independent management systems prevail over joint management systems as other studies have found both to exist in higher income groups. It is necessary, but not sufficient, for both partners to have their own income. The high incidence of this type of arrangement in my study makes it possible to shed light on some possible explanations.

Both joint and independent systems are distributed fairly evenly across the categories of living arrangement in my study (see Table 6.1). The three living arrangements which have a kitty for essentials and/or food are all in the category of multiple adult living arrangements. One of these, the urban collective [19], also has a partial pool. The partial pool is within one couple (Laura and Chris); the kitty is between all members of the arrangement. What the kitty is used for in any given arrangement varies and is related to the social relations involved in eating.

A common explanation of independent management systems is that the system tends to occur among childless and/or cohabiting couples (Pahl, 1989, p. 106; Jowell, Witherspoon and Brook, 1987; Morris, 1989, p. 455; Blumstein and Schwartz, 1983). The existence of children does not appear to make a significant difference to the distribution (see Table 6.2). Although the proportion who have children amongst those living arrangements using joint management systems is greater than that amongst those using independent management systems, of all the living arrangements with children only one-third use a joint management system. Even if single mothers are disregarded, although independence (financial and otherwise) is clearly important to their choice of living arrangement, only half of the remaining living arrangements with children use a joint management system. Rosanna Hertz (1986) reports a similar lack of relationship between children and allocative system in her study of dual-career couples.

Table 6.1: Distribution of systems of management by type of arrangement

Type of arrangement	Joint management	Independent management	
		Total	Partial pool
Single mothers by choice	0	4	0
Voluntarily childless heterosexual couples	2	3	0
Heterosexual couples with children in role reversals	3	2	0
Heterosexual couples with children with shared roles	2	2	2
Multiple adult arrangements	1	4	2
'Other'	0	2	0
Total	8	17	4

Table 6.2: Distribution of systems of management by existence of children

System		No children	Children
Joint management		2	6
Independent management	Total	6	11
	(Partial pool)	(1)	(3)
Total		8	17

Marriage seems much more significant, especially in relation to joint management systems, with no unmarried heterosexual couples using joint management (see Table 6.3). I have shown in Chapter 2 that marriage may be part of the political project. Although not marrying was important for some, others who married tried to give it new meanings using tactics like keeping their own names, not telling people that they were married, etc. This different attitude to marriage is seen again here. Many of the couples using a joint management system talked of their relationships in terms of partnership. A quote from the lesbian couple (who also used a joint management system) illustrates the idea:

> I think once you have children and *it's a joint venture* it seems a bit pointless having separate bank accounts.
>
> (Kathryn [28]; emphasis added)

This interpretation is supported by evidence from Rosanna Hertz's study of American dual-earner marriage. Her sample of 21 married couples was divided about evenly between joint and independent management systems.

Table 6.3: Distribution of systems of management by marital status

System		Married	Unmarried	No couples in arrangement
Joint management		8	0	0
Independent management	Total	5	6	6
	(Partial pool)	(2)	(2)	(0)
Total		13	6	6

Hertz found that those who pooled their incomes described marriage as 'the merger of two individuals based on unlimited trust'. They did not refer to autonomy in their discussion of trust. In contrast, those who used independent management systems didn't speak of trust but rather autonomy and retaining individual control (Hertz, 1992, pp. 142–3; see also Hertz, 1986).

It would seem that a commitment to equality and independence is an important reason for choosing the independent management system. As both Carol Burgoyne and Rosanna Hertz point out, women's contributions to the aggregate income must remain visible if they are to contribute to a more equitable distribution of power. An independent management system maintains this visibility 'so that the allocation system becomes a kind of "internal representation" of the couple's extra-familial roles' (Burgoyne, 1990, p. 638; Hertz, 1986, p. 93). Independence was certainly an important factor in the choice of living arrangement (which entailed a financial arrangement) for the four single mothers by choice and the one voluntarily childless single woman. All but one of those using an independent management system and living with other adults mentioned independence, especially for the woman, as an important part of their relationship.

Joint Management

Four of the couples who use a joint management system do not mention independence as important but there are four couples for whom this may be an issue. Three of the four have a major difference in income: the joint management system seems to be used as a way of balancing out financial inequalities. It would appear both from Hertz's evidence and the evidence in my study that the tendency towards a joint management system for married couples is overridden by the importance of independence except where the minimum condition of independent incomes is not met. Peg [7], the only woman still not accounted for, explained their choice as the 'fairest' system. Her independence appeared to be maintained by the fact that she was *able* to support herself on her income.

Regardless of whether they explicitly mention independence as important, the overwhelming evidence of the study is that dependence is not
desirable to the extent that it reproduces sexist social relations. Three of the
eight living arrangements who use a joint management system have
approximately equal incomes (Peg and Ian [7], Paula and Rob [15], and
Carolyn and Roger [17]). Of those with wide income disparities only one has
the man earning the higher income (Karen and Pete [6]).

Does a joint management system mask continuing inequalities? Amy and
Kathryn [28] are aware that this possibility exists in heterosexual relationships.

> I'm also not sure. If I lived with a man, I think I might feel
> differently. I think it's much easier for us as two women because
> there's actually a very strong commitment to quite real equality and
> [. . .] we start from a base point of equality.
>
> (Amy)

For the role reversals with joint managements systems (Liz and Steve [10],
Rebecca and Jack [12], Carol and Patrick [14], and Lynne and Dave [21]) the
contradiction between men's power as men and women's power as earners
(added to the commitment of the men to anti-sexism) reduces the potential
problems of a joint management system.

For those with approximately equal incomes, the potential problems are
more difficult to detect. It is possible that men still have more power in
spending decisions or more access to money. Owing to the variety of
information sought in the interview, I do not have enough detailed
information either to confirm or deny that this was the case. Peg [7] reported
that they meet regularly to 'do the books', never spend money without the
other one knowing and have never fought about money. Paula and Rob [15]
make most purchases together and agree a sum for gifts.

In the case of Karen and Pete [6], the potential problems are evident.
Although they are married, Karen has kept her own name, they don't wear
rings, and they don't usually tell other people. Karen has a career but it
doesn't currently bring in any money. She told me that all money is shared
equally and they have a joint account. Pete said that they made most buying
decisions in common, although a few sarcastic comments by Karen hint at
power struggles. Pete also told me that he has to try quite hard to make the
money situation not oppressive and neither of them is satisfied with it. Money
and financial dependency occasionally come up in arguments. Pete stresses
that it is not the arrangement itself they don't like but the way it makes them
feel: it gives them both something to be unhappy about.

The difficulties of resisting and rejecting the dependent nature of wife have led Karen to train for a paid job. However, there will still be a major difference in their incomes and (I assume from the comment about not disliking the arrangement itself) they will still use a joint management system. Although this is an isolated example, it indicates the difficulty of overcoming the social relations of wife and breadwinner where men are still the major earners. There is also some evidence to support this claim in Carol Burgoyne's study (1990, p. 655).

Money and Power

I would argue that the allocation of financial resources by independent management system is one way in which the role/identity of wife is resisted and rejected. In much of the literature on household allocative systems there is an attempt to flesh out the relationship between money and power. A link is made between earning and controlling household income and between control of money and power in marriage. However, there is some evidence that when the woman is the major earner, the relationship does not hold (Stamp, 1985).

> ... there is a pattern of the balance of power shifting towards the wife
> — but not too far.... For the wives in particular seemed to be trying
> to equalise the relationships, trying to avoid having too much power.
>
> (Stamp, 1985, p. 554)

Vogler and Pahl (1994) have explored this issue in more detail using data from a large survey. They show that differences in power and inequalities vary between equality and greater male power. The latter may be found where men explicitly control the finances or in low-income households with nominal female control where women experience higher levels of personal deprivation than their husbands.

The theory which informs my work suggests that power is at least partially due to the fact that men are *men*. Money may serve to reinforce or justify this position in a society based on a money economy. Money may also be used to counteract women's powerless position although there is evidence in the work of Brannen and Moss (1991) and Hochschild (1989) of the way income differences are *constructed* by couples to maintain the roles/identities of female wife and male breadwinner. In Hertz's study this was especially true for those with joint management systems (1986, pp. 84–113; 1992, pp. 141–3).

Dealing with External Constraints

Of course the ability to contribute to aggregate income and the relative contribution of men and women is not completely in the control of the individual. The labour market is heavily segregated and women's average earnings (even when controlled for hours worked) are significantly lower than men's. There is some evidence in my study of attempts to mitigate these external constraints. In contrast with many dual-earner couples with conventional ideologies who emphasize the inequality of their contributions and the greater importance of the man's income even when the 'objective' situation is not unequal (e.g. Brannen and Moss, 1991, pp. 81–9), those in my study whose incomes are unequal use various methods to create an equitable division of expenses.

A joint management system is one method but there are also several ways that those using independent management can mitigate externally imposed inequalities. Some do not try to balance the inequality; they pay equal amounts of the expenses regardless of income. Others, who pay an equal proportion of expenses in principle, do some small things which balance the situation out somewhat. In some cases it is that the one with the higher income pays for meals out or other luxury items. In the case of the rural collective [23], the woman with the lowest income, Mary, has three children. For the purposes of calculating contributions for food (which are in principle divided equally), the children are counted as one adult even though everyone recognizes that they consume more food than that. Of those who do not operate on the principle of equal payments (but rather equitable payments), there are two primary methods: paying proportions of expenses commensurate with earnings, and taking responsibility for different expenses (divided unevenly based on earnings). Table 6.4 summarizes the strategies.

Like all tables, this one simplifies things a bit too much. One couple who pay proportionally into the pool do so commensurate with responsibilities

Table 6.4: How those with independent management systems deal with unequal incomes

	Income variation		Total
	Major	Minor	
Equal proportion of expenses	1	2	3
Minor adjustments	1	2	3
Unequal proportion into pool	1	1	2
Different bills	3	0	3
No sharing of finances	0	1	1

not income. Alice [16] already had children when her relationship with Roy started and they had two more together. She received some maintenance from the father of one of her children and did not consider Roy to be financially responsible for her children though he clearly had other responsibilities of 'social' fatherhood. Jean and Eric [18] do not balance the minor variations in their incomes because their incomes fluctuate and tend to be about equal over longer periods of time. If one person is a bit short one month that individual must make do.

Conclusions

The ability to earn money can contribute to the resistance to and rejection of the role/identity of wife. This role/identity is a dependent one, thus access to an independent income (especially for women) is an important component of anti-sexist living arrangements. As studies of conventional dual-earner couples have shown, access is insufficient (see e.g. Brannen and Moss, 1991; Hertz, 1986). The high incidence of independent systems of money management is indicative of the active way in which the role/identity of wife is being resisted by those who took part in this study.

The rarity of the independent management system in the general population has led to its exclusion from much of the discussion of financial allocation within living arrangements (e.g. Vogler and Pahl, 1993, 1994). Lydia Morris argues that its complete absence in some studies may be due to 'a tendency for research to focus on the lower levels of the socio-economic scale' (1990, p. 115). I would add that the focus on married couples also obscures important factors in the allocation of money. It is now common-place to recognize that 'jointness' may be more an ideology of marriage than an adequate representation of the financial situation and may mask continu-ing inequalities.

The evidence from my research indicates that the importance of women's independence may result in the use of an independent management system. The fact that some of the women in the study also lived in non-marital and/or non-couple households may also be important. It is impossible to know whether independent management of finances results from the form of living arrange-ment or rather the difficulty of reconciling the 'joint' character of a couple/ marriage with the 'independence' of money. Thus the latter could have contributed to the decision to form a different living arrangement. Certainly Vogler and Pahl found that wives' normative attitudes about breadwinning and housework were insignificant to the system of financial allocation used (1993, p. 90) while men's normative attitudes about breadwinning were very important 'both in determining the allocatory system couples use and in mediating the relation between allocative systems and other variables' (1993, p. 91).

Notes

1   The literature has focused on households but the same could probably be said for families and resource distribution between households. Other research (e.g. Charles and Kerr, 1988) has found similar patterns in the distribution of other resources, particularly food.
2   If the wage earner is also the one who manages the money, personal spending money is not always given. See particularly the work of Pahl (1985) and Homer *et al.* (1985) on battered women.
3   Only Kate had received any maintenance from a child's father. During this time she had no contact with him apart from receiving cheques in the post so I assume that she had total control over this money.
4   I have used the term aggregate income instead of household income to avoid some of the problems that the term 'household' poses for my sample (see Chapter 1).

Chapter 7

Refusing to be a wife!

I embarked on this project motivated by an interest in feminist politics and a personal desire not to live in a conventional nuclear family household. My two primary aims were to further the understanding of the oppression of women in our society by studying an exceptional case, and to examine the political strategy of 'lifestyle politics'. My aims were addressed by considering the question, 'What are *anti-sexist* living arrangements and how far are they possible?'. My answer to this question was framed by an interpretation of feminist theories and based on an analysis of several themes which stood out in the interviews. I concluded that the defining characteristic of anti-sexist living arrangements was the refusal to be a wife. In this chapter I will review the evidence focusing on the roles and identities of wife, mother and worker. This will be followed by a consideration of the shape of anti-sexist living arrangements and how that might affect the ability to refuse wifehood. I will conclude by offering some thoughts on the implications of my findings for both feminist politics and sociological research.

I remind the reader that the analysis focused on women. Although there were interesting questions about men, masculinity and related topics, these were not explored in detail. My topic was the oppression of women and strategies for ending it. Men are considered through the manner and extent to which they participate in (or constrain) those strategies.

Summary

Wife

In support of the theoretical proposition that the role/identity of wife is central to women's oppression, I found that the characteristic common to the varied living arrangements studied was rejection of (aspects of) this role/ identity. Many of the women who participated in my study were not married. Some of these were in cohabiting heterosexual couples but others had chosen to live alone, only with their children or in a larger residential group (with or without men). Of those who were married, many had not taken their husband's name (a traditional symbol of the subordination of women) and two did not advertise their marital status. Whether in heterosexual couples (married or cohabiting) or not, there was a general rejection of the status of 'head of household' amongst the participants.

The rejection of these formal aspects of the role/identity of wife was constrained in several ways. Immigration law made it necessary for one couple with differing nationalities to marry in order to live in the same country. In addition, several participants spoke of social pressure to marry, take their husband's name or live together coming from specific persons (usually parents or siblings) or from a vague sense of it being the normal thing to do. These pressures were often described as being more difficult to overcome than one might imagine if considered in the abstract and indicated to me that even seemingly minor aspects of women's domestic roles/ identities are central to their position in society.

There was also evidence of the rejection of the appropriation of women's unpaid labour (namely housework), often through a general strategy of increasing the amount of housework for which members of living arrange- ments were individually responsible. Most commonly this included laundry, eating and related activities, and cleaning individual space (e.g. bedrooms). The residential arrangement could be critical here as single-person living arrangements could maximize individual responsibility. To a certain extent the single mothers in this study could be understood to be using this strategy. Individual responsibility was also increased through a re-evaluation of the abilities of young children who were often encouraged to do things for themselves.

Two strategies for dealing with communal responsibilities were found: the 'swap', in which all tasks were divided and assigned to individuals; and 'sharing', in which all tasks were done by all members perhaps alternating equally over time. Both strategies highlight different aspects of the traditional division of housework. The swap emphasizes the usual lack of a standard of equivalence; sharing, the hierarchical nature of decision making (particularly evident in debates about standards). Comparison with other research led to the conclusion that all three strategies were constrained by a reliance on men's willingness to negotiate an equal division of housework (or, in the case of single mothers, not to interfere in the running of the living arrangement). The analysis also raised questions about the social relations governing paid domestic work although the data were insufficient to address them.

The economic aspects of the role/identity of wife were also actively resisted and rejected. Delphy and Leonard (1992) emphasize the difference between a wage and maintenance arguing that the latter is characteristic of husband–wife relations. The high incidence of independent financial management amongst the participants indicates the rejection of the maintained status of wife. This form of resistance was constrained by access to an independent income but there were a few cases where both partners had such access and an independent management system was not used. In these cases an ideology of partnership was usually important. Where a joint management system was used to compensate for major differences in income, the woman was usually earning the larger (or only) income, a fact which counteracted the gendered nature of power in the household. In the one case where a man financially supported a woman, it was found to be difficult to maintain equality. The rejection of maintenance was also inherent in some of the formal aspects outlined above, especially for women not living in couples. The ability to undertake this sort of resistance is similarly dependent on access to an independent income although, in addition, it must be large enough to cover the costs of living alone or parenting alone.

The use of independent management systems can also be understood as the rejection of the appropriation of women's paid labour. Research has shown that women's paid work is often used to supplement *household* income and contributes to the maintenance of the house and children. Even when employed, women rarely have access to or control over substantial discretionary income. By maintaining independent control of their income women's contributions to common expenditure remain visible and access to and control of (at least some of) any discretionary income is made possible.

Mother

The rejection of the role/identity of wife had implications for the other two roles/identities. The analysis of mothering revealed that the participants were trying to separate in practice what I (and other feminist theorists) have separated analytically — the two domestic roles of women. This separation was evident in the importance of choice to some of those in the study. Choice was found to be more important in the negative, positive choices to mother (or have children) only being found amongst those not usually expected to do so (e.g. single women, lesbians). This was understood to be a reflection of the comparative difficulty of redefining the meaning of a social role as opposed to rejecting a social expectation.

For those in heterosexual couples with children there was evidence of attempting to change the conditions in which mothering took place and the practice of mothering despite the apparent taken-for-granted character of having children. In particular, the negotiation of a balance between non-domestic work and mothering (found in most categories) indicates a change from the expectation that mothering should be of primary importance. There were also examples of men assuming the role/identity of mother. More generally, for those with children, mothering took on a political character as evidenced by anti-sexist child-rearing strategies and their influence, through the importance of role-models, on adult behaviour.

Constraints on these strategies lay again in the reliance on men accepting women's choices (and, in the case of single women and lesbians, being willing biologically to father a child without assuming the authority of a father over the woman and her children). Participants also stressed the importance of practical, emotional and political support. Practical support was usually in the form of child-care and women in couples often relied on their partners. The lack of political support for the choices participants had made had an impact here in that it made it difficult for men to take an equal role or limited the extent of practical support to women in unconventional living arrangements. Political attacks (e.g. on single mothers, lesbian mothers or working mothers), whether general or personal, also fed anxiety about whether they were doing the best for their children.

Worker

Participants (men and women) also rejected the role/identity of worker. Most sought flexibility in employment in order to accommodate their domestic responsibilities and other non-domestic interests. They characterized non-domestic work as (ideally) meeting their needs. This was particularly true of flexibility but also of the type of work. They also rejected the pursuit of more and more money as a goal of non-domestic work. Some spoke of work as primarily for bringing in money and many talked of settling for less money or bringing in 'enough' money. Many could have been earning more than they were and some had taken a cut in salary or a 'backwards step' for reasons related to their living arrangement. Constraints were most evident when comparing the occupations of members of different living arrange-ments. Those most likely to have flexible work were in teaching, social services or politically aware organizations but even in these areas consider-able variation was found.

The Shape of Anti-sexist Living Arrangements

Although, following Dorothy Smith (1990), I was not concerned with the typicality of my sample because even atypical stories bear the traces of the social organization and relations in which they are located, I did construct the sample to ensure groupings of similar living arrangements. In doing so I hoped to be able to draw some conclusions about the advantages and disadvantages, and the enabling or constraining effects of particular arrangements. What effect does a particular living arrangement have on the distribution of power? Can any living arrangement be anti-sexist if the will is there? Are people constrained (externally) to arrange their lives in particular ways?

The respondents were characterized as primarily white, middle-class, well-educated and heterosexual. I speculated on why this might have been the case and concluded that these characteristics limited the extent of constraints on individual action. This is particularly relevant in the consideration of external constraints and the importance of access to well-paid, flexible non-domestic work. This access was not straightforward but could be assumed to be easier given the specific characteristics of the respondents and the well-documented racism (and classism) in British education and the labour market. Regarding sexuality, the situation was more complex. It was suggested that the meaning of (hetero)sexuality varied with living arrangements and that the existence of a couple relationship (and its character) was an important factor. These issues have been incorporated into the comparison of various arrangements in terms of the distribution of power.

When planning the project I thought it would be useful to have a preliminary categorization of possible types of living arrangement. My initial categorization into six groups was based on the number of adults in an arrangement (one, two, more than two) and whether or not there were children. This was later modified when I realized that sexuality was important to the character of a two-adult living arrangement and that there were several ways such an arrangement could be organized. These issues will form the structure of this section.

Size

In comparing living arrangements of different sizes one finds that external constraints impact differently according to this criterion. For those in living arrangements with a single adult, costs were proportionately greater, practical support was more complicated to arrange, and flexibility of non-domestic work was more important. These factors were particularly obvious in the comparison of single mothers who lived only with their children and those who were in multiple adult arrangements.

This comparison also highlights the conceptual difficulties of defining the boundaries of a living arrangement and the hegemony of the concept of the 'household'. People generally spoke about their living arrangements in relation to one residential group. However, Kate's [1]¹ situation when her first child was very young, for example, could be understood as a multiple adult living arrangement spanning two residential groups, particularly in terms of the practical, emotional and political support which her mother and sister provided.

The size of the residential group also had an impact on the division of housework. For single adult residential groups individual responsibility could be maximized as communal space was minimal. Since the traditional division of housework is based on a two-adult household, larger groups were likely to need to negotiate the division. This may not be the case for large kin-based residential groups where a head of household may still appropriate the labour of his dependants (see Delphy and Leonard, 1992) but the assignment of the status of head of household in large non-kin residential groups is perhaps more problematic.

Children

The most obvious difference between living arrangements with children and those without was men's attitude to non-domestic work. Childless men who rejected the role/identity of worker were only found in the two collectives. Although having children does not inevitably lead men to anti-sexist ways of living, the importance of contributing equally to their care and providing them with new role models does seem to have a broader impact on men's lives. It should also be considered that living arrangements with children have larger amounts of housework (at least for certain periods) which might make the role of worker unsustainable. Thus men in voluntarily childless heterosexual couples could do their share of the housework (often further reduced by the employment of a cleaner) without impinging on the primacy of their non-domestic work. Having children also had an impact on women by highlighting the importance of non-domestic work and the difficulty of striking the right balance between non-domestic work and mothering.

Types of Couple Relationship

I separated the heterosexual couples into three groups: those who were voluntarily childless; those who had reversed roles; and those with shared roles. The three groups differed noticeably in their resistance to the formal aspects of the role/identity of wife. While heterosexual couples with children with shared roles had quite diverse practices regarding marriage and names, those in role reversals were primarily married and had taken the man's name. Voluntarily childless heterosexual couples were usually married but had kept their own names and may have gone further to avoid advertising their marital status.

The differences between the two categories of heterosexual couples with children were primarily in women's relationship to non-domestic work, the division of housework and the external constraint placed by the availability of flexible employment. While there were some who had clearly chosen a role-reversal, the nature of external constraints limited that choice for many. The same external factors also affected the extent to which roles were shared in shared-role arrangements although this was often seen as temporary. The major factor here was the availability of well-paid part-time (or other flexible) non-domestic work for both partners. This external situation influenced the extent to which the role/identity of worker was rejected. Men in both categories, and women in shared-role living arrangements, could be understood to have rejected it (for themselves at least) but women in role reversals seemed not to have done so. The division of housework differed correspondingly with shared-role living arrangements negotiating an equal division and role reversals approaching a 'true' reversal of traditional responsibilities (in marked contrast with those in other studies).

Men

One criticism of my initial categorization that led to the modification of the categories was the variety of two-adult living arrangements. The final categorization took account of the possibility of different types of couples but did not adequately account for two-adult non-couple living arrangements. In addition, the gender composition of non-couple living arrangements was not a criterion for categorization. I changed the name of one category from 'single *parents* by choice' to 'single *mothers* by choice' to reflect the *de facto* composition of the category but the multiple adult category remained mixed. The living arrangements studied can be divided between those with men and those without. This division aligns with other factors as most of the men in the study were in (heterosexual) couples while many of the women in living arrangements without men were not in couples.

The division of housework is clearly affected by the gender of members of the living arrangement. At a basic level, those in heterosexual couples often spoke of different knowledge and abilities related to gender (and socialization). These differences may be accommodated or overcome but they impact on the eventual division. At a more abstract level, as Sarah F. Berk (1985) points out, the production of gender is implicated in the production of household goods and services in heterosexual living arrangements. Thus trying to produce *only* household goods and services will involve confronting the production of gender. Comparison with other studies has shown the rarity of men's commitment to an equal division of housework. I have, therefore, treated reliance on the commitment of men as a constraint on anti-sexist living arrangements.

Again, one should not confuse living arrangements with residential groups. Those living arrangements in my study which did not have male members were certainly atypical in that they had little involvement with men (or at least men had little or no impact on the organization of the living arrangement). The biological fathers of any children were unknown or uninterested. This atypicality could be understood as a reliance on men not assuming the powerful role/identity available to them. However, living arrangements without men have the advantage of not having to struggle with the nature of cross-gender interaction on a daily (hourly) basis.

This distinction was also evident in the analysis of mothering where there was evidence of negative sanctions on men for rejecting the role/identity of worker and assuming a multi-faceted identity which included a strong commitment to mothering and housework. The difficulty of getting the necessary practical, emotional and political support indicates both the constraint on anti-sexist living arrangements and the likely importance of that support taken for granted in conventional living arrangements. Negative sanctions were also in evidence for those who had decided to mother without men, as practical and emotional support was made contingent on de-emphasizing the political nature of the chosen living arrangement. Changes in social security regulations (especially the introduction of the Child Support Agency) since the interviews took place could also have an impact on the ability to form certain types of anti-sexist living arrangements.

Implications for Feminist Political Strategies

The analysis of the material in this (albeit small) study indicates some possible directions for feminist politics. On a general level, 'lifestyle politics' are seen to have a role although the limits imposed by the organization of the public sphere indicate that a 'public' politics is also necessary. More specifically I see three areas for which the study has implications.

First, the comparison of living arrangements with and without male members indicates the necessity for a re-evaluation of the politics of separation. In making this claim I am drawing on Marilyn Frye's definition of 'feminist separation' —

> Feminist separation is, of course, separation of various sorts or modes from men and from institutions, relationships, roles and activities which are male-defined, male-dominated and operating for the benefit of males and the maintenance of male privilege — this separation being initiated or maintained, at will, *by women*. (Masculist separatism is the partial segregation of women from men and male domains *at the will of men*. This difference is crucial.)
>
> (Frye, 1983c, p. 96; original emphasis)[2]

— and her distinction between 'feminist separation' and 'feminist separatism' —

> Most feminists, probably all, practice some separation from males and male-dominated institutions. A separatist practices separation consciously, systematically, and probably more generally than the others, and advocates thorough and 'broad spectrum' separation as part of the conscious strategy of liberation.
>
> (Frye, 1983c, p. 98)

She discusses the ways in which women controlling male access to ourselves is a way of taking power and of redefining the category 'woman', a process which implies a redefinition of 'man' (see Frye, 1983c, pp. 105–7).[3] In the context of my research, feminist separation is implied in the rejection of the role/identity of wife.

As feminists we should be encouraging such separation. We must also recognize that there are multiple ways in which feminist separation may be attempted. Some women may choose to have little or nothing to do with men in any sphere of their lives (separatism). Others may choose to maintain close sexual and affective ties with men but not live with them. The problems of support experienced by some of the women in the study indicate that alternative support networks must be created in order for these strategies to be successful. Feminist support for feminist separation involves creating and maintaining such networks, and fighting for access to resources for 'separated' women.

Second, the way that the creation of anti-sexist living arrangements was constrained by the organization of non-domestic work, and the role/identity of worker was rejected by many of the participants has implications for feminist political strategies in the workplace. In particular, the need for well-paid, flexible work which meets the needs of workers (as opposed to the current rhetoric of a cheap, flexible workforce to meet the needs of employers) seems important. Support for part-time workers by trade unions would form part of this strategy as well as providing support crucial to the success of anti-sexist living arrangements.

The reorganization of non-domestic work is also necessary if dependence on low-paid women as domestic workers is to be avoided. Rosanna Hertz (1986) notes that for the corporate couples she studied, the construction of worker was not challenged and their strategies were only possible because they could employ domestic workers at low wages. Similarly, socialist demands for the collectivization of domestic work have rarely addressed the question of who would be doing it in what conditions.[4] The current construction of the worker does not even allow for the individual taking responsibility for his own needs (e.g. for food, clean clothes), assuming he[5] has a wife (or wife substitute) to take care of them. The integration of care of others (e.g. young children, the ill, the elderly) requires revolutionary changes in the organization of both the public and the private spheres. The strategies followed by those with children in my study provide an indication of the possible direction of change. This includes the need for support in the form of collective care but does not see that collective care as 'freeing' women (or men) to be 'workers'.

Third, the attempts by many of those in my study to separate in practice what some theorists have separated analytically — the role/identity of mother from that of wife — indicates the potential for transforming mothering from something 'self-sacrificing and powerless' to 'a really wonderful experience to go through' (Kathryn [28]). I would argue that mothering as a distinct role/identity should be integrated into feminist strategies. We would then be able to build on the existing motivations of many women and men to transform their relationships.[6] Miriam Johnson (1988) argues further that mothering, freed from wifehood, could form the basis of a non-oppressive society. Other studies suggest that practical involvement in mothering has the potential to challenge men's relationship to non-domestic work as well as domestic responsibility (e.g. Coltrane, 1989). Although this should not be exaggerated, feminists must be able to build on that potential.

The dangers of focusing on motherhood are numerous (see Delphy, 1992). However, although some feminists base their evaluation of mothering on women's specificity, it does not have to rest on such an essentialist construction. Johnson argues that mothering freed from wifehood would rest on values of interdependence which would respect the autonomy of each instead of those of dependence and independence. Of course we cannot know what mothering would look like in these conditions. However, the value that the participants in my study placed on children's autonomy (e.g. encouraging them to take individual responsibility for some of the tasks necessary to their care and survival) indicate that interdependence may indeed be the result. These values are social ones encouraged by the practice of nurturing and may provide the basis for a rejection of essentialist notions of mothering which imply the 'ownership' of children.[7]

Carole Pateman's (1988) revelation that the original stories on which contract theory (which she argues always creates relations of domination and subordination) rely are based on relations between adult males and are incapable of incorporating the care of infants suggest that this interpretation may have some possibilities. We do not need new original stories but our ability to imagine different social relations forms one part of a wider strategy to transform society.[8]

Implications for Sociological Research

The whole project was conceived as part of the 'feminist revolution in sociology' which would involve '(1) the transformation of existing conceptual frameworks; and (2) the acceptance of those transformations by others in the field' (Stacey and Thorne, 1985, p. 302). My work was located within a feminist sociological tradition which is asking feminist questions as well as providing feminist answers to (conventional) sociological questions. By framing my question in an explicitly political way, two possible conceptual improvements were highlighted.

The first relates to the terminology used in sociological research in the domestic sphere. After reviewing definitions of 'family' and 'household', it was decided that both had limitations from both a sociological and feminist standpoint. Although definitions of 'family' are in the process of being challenged as a political response to the recognition of a variety of living arrangements, the new definitions have limited usefulness for sociological categorization. Some researchers, recognizing this, have decided to focus on households instead but this term still incorporates assumptions of communality, and sometimes equality and consensus, which have been questioned by sociological research. I chose the terms 'living arrangement' and 'residential group' as offering the possibility of problematizing both the extent to which communality forms part of the arrangement being studied, and the membership of the group (including the character of relationships between members). I also hoped to avoid the all too frequent elision of 'family' and 'household'.

This proved difficult in practice as the terms have a popular currency in our society. The politics of definition extend beyond the control of the sociological researcher. However, if the research process is understood as a political one, then struggling to apply these concepts becomes a possibility. What aspects of domestic life become visible if we move away from a focus on 'family' and 'household' to 'living arrangements' and 'residential groups'? I am suggesting a broader field than the existing research on the use of the term 'family' by individuals to describe their living arrangements. How often are samples based on criteria including 'married couples with at least one child under 16 years of age'? What effect does this have on the results? Would problematizing the form of domestic organization (within and beyond 'households') improve our understanding of the division of labour, the allocation of resources, and the relationship between the public and the private? Research on the importance of social networks to employment status (for example) indicates that it might.

The second possible conceptual improvement is the analytical separation of the domestic roles of women. Many studies of the domestic division of labour and of women's position in the labour market have observed a link between women's responsibility for child-care, their responsibility for housework and their particular location in the labour market/force. I have suggested that the separation of the role/identity of wife, which includes primary domestic responsibility and involvement in non-domestic work as a supplement to the husband's income, from that of mother is useful to understand the oppositional character of anti-sexist living arrangements. A few studies of conventional living arrangements without children have noted that the gendered division of labour develops early in marriage (e.g. Mansfield and Collard, 1988). The relationship between mothering and the oppression of women could be clarified if the two roles/identities were separated systematically in analysis. Does a relationship to a child make women vulnerable to subordination? Or is it more directly implicated in the gendering of the division of labour (as assumed by theorists such as Parsons)?

The analytical separation of the domestic roles of women is difficult without the possibility of comparison of different living arrangements. Thus the possibility that it is not responsibility for children but the understanding of the role/identity of wife which leads to women's primary responsibility for housework and its impact on their non-domestic work is only observable when studies of childless married couples are conducted. In addition, by focusing on 'living arrangements', sexual relations between members cannot be assumed. What impact do they have on the organization of living arrangements?

My study has also highlighted the impact of beliefs on domestic organization. Although I have focused on feminist beliefs, the impact of other beliefs (e.g. religious) on the family may warrant study particularly as they interact with pragmatic and structural factors. These conceptual modifications would refocus traditional sociological questions and improve our understanding of the social relations governing different living arrangements and the extent to which individuals (can) contribute to the construction and reconstruction of gender relations.

Notes

1   The numbers in parentheses refer to the participants list in Appendix 1.
2   This latter distinction is similar to the one Janice Raymond makes between 'sex-separated' and 'sex-segregated'. Raymond makes an additional point; sex-segregated women may become sex-separated (1991, p. 143).
3   See also her essays on 'Sexism' and 'To See and Be Seen: The Politics of Reality' in the same volume. Her metaphor of foreground/background, actor/stagehand in the latter is particularly illuminating.
4   This is in addition to the problem raised by Delphy and Leonard (1992) of the qualitative difference between individual and collective service.
5   The use of the masculine pronoun is intentional.
6   The participants in my study were often motivated by the perceived needs of their children.
7   I am addressing Delphy's (1992) criticisms here. She has focused on only one aspect of feminist writing about motherhood but, to the extent that it exists, it is a worrying one.
8   See Charlotte Perkins Gilman's *Herland* (1979) for an example of an imagined society based on motherhood as a social relationship. It is interesting that she imagines this as a society without men.

The Participants

A brief description of each of the living arrangements studied is given in this appendix. Indicative information on standard of living is included, though not necessarily precise incomes. Names have been changed, and geographical locations not specified, in order to protect the confidentiality of the interviews. Details of how I chose these people and the geographical distribution and general characteristics of the sample are found in Appendix 2. For ease of reference, living arrangements are numbered and the numbers are used with the names in the text and tables contained in the book.

Single Mothers by Choice

[1] *Kate* is a freelance scriptwriter who has also worked as a teacher both in schools and in an FE college. Her daughter, Ruth (age 20) is finishing a degree at university where she is the women's officer. Heather (age 10) still lives at home. Ruth's father made a small financial contribution until her eighteenth birthday. Kate describes her financial situation as 'precarious'. I interviewed Kate alone at her home, and Ruth at college.

[2] *Maggie* worked as a social worker when Tina (age 9) was born but now teaches social work full time in a local college. She also has two lodgers. I interviewed her in her home.

[3] *Ann* is currently a part-time worker for two housing co-operatives. She has previously worked in building co-ops and adult education. She was living in a communal housing co-op (several small houses near together) when her two boys[1] (now ages 8 and 10) were born. Since then she has lived on her own and shared a flat with another mother. She has a relatively low income although at the time of the interview a friend had moved into the flat so her fixed expenses will be shared. Ann was interviewed at home, alone.

[4] *Jane* is living in local authority housing with her daughter, Dorothy (age

3). Dorothy has a physical disability which affects her acquisition of language. Jane is unemployed and claiming Income Support. Jane was interviewed at home alone. Information from several letters (written in response to draft versions of the text) is also included.

Voluntarily Childless Heterosexual Couples

[5] *Roseanne and John* are unmarried and have lived together for 2½ years. Roseanne is a civil servant recently promoted to a management grade and earning £16500. John is a civil engineer earning £11500. They were interviewed together in their home.

[6] *Karen and Pete* have been married 10 years but don't usually tell people. She has kept her own name. Pete is a consultant with a large computer company earning a relatively high salary. Karen is a writer (unpaid) and training to be a counsellor. They were interviewed together over lunch in their home.

[7] *Peg and Ian* have been together for 13 years and are married. She has kept her own name. Peg is a health visitor. Ian is a computer programmer. Both are employed full time and earn approximately equal amounts. Peg was interviewed alone in her sister's home. She did not realize that I wanted to speak to Ian.

[8] *Louise and Mark* have been together for 12 years and married for 10. Louise has kept her own name. She is a nurse working approximately 25 hours per week for an agency. He is a full-time university lecturer currently in his first academic job having recently completed his PhD. Mark currently earns more than Louise. They were interviewed together in their home.

[9] *Barbara and Juan* have been married 4 years (because, being of different nationalities, it was necessary in order to live together) but don't usually tell people. She has kept her own name. Juan is a law student; Barbara a university lecturer. Barbara earns approximately £16000; Juan is living off his savings. They were interviewed together in a restaurant.

Heterosexual Couples with Children in Role-reversal Situations

[10] *Liz and Steve* have been together 13 years (married for 10) and have two daughters (ages 7 and 5). Liz is a social worker earning approximately £17000 and is doing an MA part time. Steve was a tool setter/operator with an engineering firm before becoming a full-time father. They were interviewed together in their home.

[11] *Christiane and Wilhelm* have been married 4 years and have two sons (ages 1½ and 3). Christiane is an accountant currently working full time. Wilhelm is currently taking 16 months' unpaid leave from his job as an executive with a computer company. His salary is in excess of £200000 and he has been able to keep some benefits (pension, car) while on leave. They are European and have been living in England for 3 years. They were interviewed together in their home.

[12] *Rebecca and Jack* are married and have a daughter (age 7). Rebecca has been promoted to a management position with the local library and earns about £14000. Jack worked in a bookshop then left to pursue artistic interests. He now works part time in a supermarket, plays in a band and writes children's books with a friend. He earns about £3000. They were interviewed together in their home. One picked me up from the station and the other took me back allowing some conversation with each of them individually (not taped).

[13] *Linda and Dan* are now separated after a 7-year relationship. Their two children (ages 9 and 6) live with Dan although when they first separated they lived with Linda. Linda works as a secretary for a trade union and has two lodgers. Dan previously worked as an engineer and is now a full-time father claiming Income Support. Linda was interviewed in a restaurant. Dan was interviewed at a later date in his home.

[14] *Carol and Patrick* have been married 12 years. She has kept her own name for work purposes, their two children (ages 5 and 4) have his name. Carol has recently set up her own business as a media consultant after 25 years as a civil servant. She earns approximately £29500. Patrick has worked in various jobs but immediately before becoming a full-time father he was a management trainee with a large group of companies. Carol was interviewed in her office. Patrick did not want to participate in the research.

Heterosexual Couples with Children with Shared Roles

[15] *Carolyn and Roger* have been married for 9 years. Carolyn has kept her name and their 3 children (ages 6, 4 and 4 months) have her name. Carolyn has a DPhil and has recently found part-time lecturing work at a local university with a salary of approximately £8000. Roger has a TEFL qualification and has been teaching full and part time. Their combined income in the previous year was about £12000. Carolyn and Roger were interviewed together in their home. I stayed the night and spoke informally to Carolyn over breakfast (not taped).

[16] *Alice and Roy* have been living together for about 15 years. Alice has

two children from previous relationships (now ages 24 and 18) and she and Roy have two children (ages 12 and 8). Roy works part time as a teacher in a boys' school (varying from 4 to 2½ days per week). Alice did social work and teaching part time when the children were younger and full time for 8 years. She has been director of a psychiatric unit for 2 years now, for which she has a relatively high salary (£25 000 approx). Alice has also been actively involved in voluntary work and was a local councillor for 4 years. They were interviewed together in their home though I arrived before Alice and spoke to Roy on his own for a while.

[17] *Paula and Rob* are married and have one son (age 3). They both work full time in social services and have worked in the voluntary, public and private sectors. Paula did work part time for about 9 months. They were interviewed together in their home.

[18] *Jean and Eric* have been married 2 years and have one child (age 6 months). Jean has kept her own name. Eric was a part-time secretary for a voluntary organization. Jean currently works part time as a development officer for a child-minding association. They both also work freelance in the voluntary sector where payment is often related to the client's ability to pay. They both are earning relatively low incomes (Jean says that if she worked full time in a community centre they would have more than their current combined income). They were interviewed together in their home.

Multiple Adult Arrangements

[19] *The urban collective* has been in the current house for 2 years. There are eight people living in this household including three couples. Five were interviewed. The other three are a couple from abroad who are working at a local university, and a single man who is an artist claiming Income Support. Laura is setting up her own accounting business from a room in the house, is writing a book and does some casual clerical work. She earns about £8000. Chris works as a researcher at a local university earning £16 700. They have been together for 3 years. Jackie and Julian (together 2½ years) are unemployed and claiming Income Support. Beth works full time for an insurance company and part time in a pub. I got the impression that the couple not interviewed were temporary. Laura, Chris, Jackie and Julian were interviewed over a meal in their home. I stayed the night and interviewed Beth in the morning (she had been working the night before).

[20] *Miriam and Sally* bought a house together 6 years ago after living in a commune for a brief period. Miriam has a child (age 8). Sally moved out about 1 year ago. Miriam's sister bought her share but has since moved as

well. There are two lodgers. Miriam works part time as a teacher in further education often combining contracts for different institutions. She earns less than if she had a permanent contract with an institution as she doesn't get paid for holidays and has no benefits. Miriam was interviewed alone in her home. I also spoke to Sally (not taped) alone in her new home afterwards.

[21] *Lynne and Dave* have been married about 13 years. She took his name but doesn't think she would now. They have five children including one from Lynne's previous marriage (age 19), one of their own (age 12), and three foster children (ages 18, 17, 13). The eldest of the foster children is officially out of care but still living with them. The placement has broken down with the other two. The foster children had been with them for 11 years. Lynne works as a researcher, often from home, and earns £17 500. Dave does a small amount of freelance building work earning £8000 (including rental income from a flat attached to the house). They have had lodgers in the past, two of whom were 'more than lodgers' and provided much needed support with three teenagers. Lynne and Dave were interviewed in their home.

[22] Val and Jason *Peterson* are married with three children (Bob, 22; Susie, 19; and Jenny, 13). Val's mother, Margaret, has been living with them for 9 years. Susie is currently away at university. They date their current arrangements (regarding division of labour, etc.) as starting about 10 years ago and evolving 'in a slow but big way'. Jason works freelance as a designer (earning about £24 000 gross) and has an office in the house. Val is a civil servant (earning £16 000) and has previously worked as a part-time researcher, often from home. Bob works full-time for a carpeting firm and often works weekends. He earns £13 500. Margaret is a widow and now receives an old-age pension in addition to money from her husband's estate. Val, Jason and Bob were interviewed in their home. Jenny was present but did not participate.

[23] At the time of the interview *the rural collective* were undergoing major changes. Two members had recently left and Mary was about to move to a flat in a nearby city although she would maintain links and continue to visit regularly. Mary is divorced and has three children (ages 11, 9, and 7) and has lived in the collective for 1½ years. She previously worked as a teacher but is currently unemployed and claiming Income Support. Sara has been living in the collective for a year and works part time (job-share) for the council in a relatively well-paid position. Eleanor owns the property and is retired. Alex has been living in the collective since it began 11 years ago, and works as a therapist. Alex, Mary and Sara were present for the interview which took place in their garden. Sara was not present for part of the interview.

Other Arrangements

[24] *Pat* is a voluntarily childless single woman. She is a writer but was previously employed as an editor for a publishing company. She currently does part-time clerical work to support herself (on a very low income though more than she would get on Income Support). Pat was interviewed in a restaurant.

[25] *Lisa* and Jim have been together for 2 years but do not live together (although they plan to at some stage). Both were previously married. She works as a teacher in a girls' secondary school. Jim is an electronics engineer. Lisa was interviewed alone in her home.

Additional Information

There are two people whom I did not interview although I have used material from their letters.

[26] *Lucy* and her male partner reversed roles when their eldest child (now age 8) was born. She is a civil servant and was earning almost double her partner's salary at that time. They now have more than one child and no longer have this arrangement.

[27] *Allison* and her male partner have been together for 13 years. They live in separate flats in the same building and spend alternate weekends together. Both work full time.

One couple who were part of the original study have been used only for comparative purposes in the book.

[28] *Amy and Kathryn* are a lesbian couple who have been together for 11 years. They have two children (ages 7 and 4). Each is the biological mother of one child. Both children have double-barrelled surnames. Currently Amy works full time in the voluntary sector. Kathryn works part time in occupational health and has previously worked full time in that field. They were interviewed together in their home over lunch. At their request I supplied them with further details of the project before the interview.

Notes

1   Ann has requested that I identify their gender from the beginning since it influences the importance she places on certain aspects of her living arrangement. Others (e.g. Amy and Kathryn) would prefer that I refer to their children as 'children' unless necessary to a specific argument. I have tried to respect their wishes and have used the latter strategy unless requested otherwise.

Appendix 2

Methods and Methodology

In this appendix I will detail the methods used as well as the characteristics of the respondents and those chosen for interview. I begin with some reflections on feminist methodology. The more specific discussion will be related to the principles of feminist research where appropriate.

Feminist Methodology

The literature on feminist methodology is vast. My own research has been most influenced by some of the work on feminist standpoint, particularly that of Sandra Harding and Dorothy Smith. However, there seem to be several versions of feminist standpoint (or standpoint of women) some of which have epistemological implications with which I disagree. I will focus here on what I understand to be the key points in most discussions of feminist method- ology and their implications. There are two main propositions common to most discussions of feminist methodology: (1) that feminism matters in research; and (2) that feminist research is *for* women.

Feminism Matters

The proposition that feminism matters has led to speculation about what feminist research might look like. Feminists have discussed appropriate topics for research, appropriate techniques of data collection and analysis, the treatment of the researched and the accessibility of their research results to non-academic women. The idea that research should be useful is reflected in explicit policy proposals, collaboration with pressure groups and action research. Myriad techniques and suggestions have been put forward many of which are hotly debated (e.g. the uses of quantitative methods).

The debates have not remained at the level of techniques. Epistemological issues were soon brought in. One of the key epistemological questions is the understanding and usefulness of 'objectivity'. One approach which rejects objectivity and the possibility of a feminist *analysis* is that of Liz Stanley and Sue Wise (1983). Their position is that 'truth' and 'objectivity' are constructions and thus all explanations (including 'scientific' explanations) are individual ones and equally valid. Stanley and Wise seem to agree with the need for a political feminist social science but they distrust methods/theories which try to go 'beyond the personal'. Margrit Eichler (1988) argues that many feminists do not find their approach helpful and have opted instead for a closer examination of objectivity leading to the rejection of aspects of its traditional definition but the retention of others. As Dorothy Smith puts it:

> ... it is essential that the everyday world be seen as organized by social relations not observable within it. Thus, an inquiry confining itself to the everyday world of direct experience is not adequate to explicate its social organization.
>
> (Smith, 1988, p. 89)

The debate over the modification or rejection of 'objectivity' is in no way resolved. However, there is a general tendency amongst feminists to reincorporate that which has been assumed to be antithetical to the achievement of objectivity in mainstream research (e.g. politics, emotions). This process has led to a re-evaluation of 'validity' and 'reliability' linked to a re-evaluation of the epistemological question of who can be a 'knower'. If women (and not just academic women) can be 'knowers', can their experiences be used to validate knowledge gained through research?

The proposition that feminism matters has also led to a critique of other research and the proposition that all research may be affected by the (usually unexamined) political stance of the researcher. In particular, feminists have drawn attention to the interest that white, middle-class men have in maintaining the status quo and the possible effects of this (implicit) political stance on their research.

Research for Women

Although there is considerable variation in the extent to which feminists argue that feminist research should be *about* women and *by* women, that feminist research is *for* women is almost universally accepted. The implications of research *for* women are primarily that questions arise from the needs of women for knowledge (as opposed to the traditional sources of questions in gaps in the literature, the needs of policy makers, etc.):

> ... the questions an oppressed group wants answered are rarely requests for so-called pure truth. Instead, they are queries about how to change its conditions; how its world is shaped by forces beyond it; how to win over, defeat, or neutralize those forces arrayed against its emancipation, growth, or development; and so forth. Consequently, feminist research projects originate primarily not in any old 'women's experiences', but in women's experiences in political struggles.
>
> (Harding, 1987, p. 8)

This returns us momentarily to the question of validity and reliability. If the questions arise out of political struggles, *political* criteria become explicit in the evaluation of feminist research:

> ... we are not grappling with notions of truth, but more simply and rudely with how to write a sociology that will somehow lay out for women, for people, how our everyday worlds are organized and how they are shaped and determined by relations that extend beyond them.
>
> (Smith, 1988, p. 121)

It is on this basis that women's experiences can be used to validate feminist knowledge. We must ask ourselves, 'Does this explanation make sense of women's lives? Does it help us/them to understand the difficulties of pursuing particular political strategies?'.

If feminist research is *for* women and women's experiences are to be used as a basis for the evaluation of the research, the dissemination of the results to women becomes necessary. This has implications for the way that the research is written and where it is published. Women's role in the evaluation of research is predicated on the acceptance of their status as 'knowers' but also leads to difficult questions concerning their role in the research process. What is the relationship between the researcher and the researched? Should the researched have input into the formulation of the questions?; the collection of the data?; the analysis of the data? These questions are particularly important when the women *for* whom the research is done are also the women *about* whom the research is done. Women criminologists have pointed out that the relationship between the researcher and the researched can be much different when the research is *about* (powerful) men yet *for* (disempowered) women (see Gelsthorpe and Morris, 1990).

Feminist Sociology

The two propositions which I have stated to be fundamental to feminist methodology taken together imply a radical transformation of the entire research process. It is not just a matter of using open-ended interviews instead of structured questionnaires, or of using different sampling methods. The more radical strands of this debate point towards a transformation of academe as a whole. It involves recognizing sociology as it is currently practised (and academe in general), as part of the ruling apparatus. Feminist sociology, on this model, challenges the relations of ruling (to use Dorothy Smith's term) and the role of academe in those relations, and rejects the privileging of the sociologist's knowledge over that of the subjects of the research.

I will deal briefly with two criticisms often made of feminist methodology which I believe to be unfounded. The first is essentialism. Arguably some feminists have an essentialist conception of 'woman'. However, this is not inherent to feminism nor to feminist methodology. The category 'woman' is conceptualized as socially constructed and its meaning is historically and culturally variable. Nevertheless, such a category does exist in our society. It is not women as biological entities but women as oppressed people in struggle against their oppression who are implied in the criteria of feminist research. It is useful to remember at this point that feminists have also sought to expand our notion of what constitutes 'struggle against their oppression'. Elizabeth Fee points out (1988) that this politicized approach is not exclusive to feminism but is/can be used by any and all oppressed groups.

The rejection of 'Truth' as the goal of research and the modification or rejection of 'objectivity' has also been misrepresented as relativist (although arguably *some* feminists take a relativist position). Dorothy Smith (1988) proposes the standpoint of women as a 'point of entry' from which to explore the social relations structuring and influencing a woman's experience. The goal is not to find 'universal truth' but to map out these relations, to explain to women how their lived experiences fit into a bigger structure. It is easy to see how some might think that any 'point of entry' would produce equally valid sociological explanations.

Sandra Harding questions the position from which the criticism of relativism is made:

Historically, relativism appears as an intellectual possibility, and as a 'problem', only for dominating groups at the point where the hegemony (the universality) of their views is being challenged.

(1987, p. 10)

As Smith (1990) demonstrates, mainstream sociology is also (implicitly) political and can use its conceptual practices (e.g. criticizing feminist standpoint as relativist) to undermine its critics. However, to question the legitimacy of the criticism is not sufficient. The introduction of *political* criteria into the evaluation of accounts is, to my mind, the most promising direction for anti-relativist feminist research.

Translating these debates into practice was not easy. I find it useful to think of myself as a researcher struggling to achieve a feminist research practice in much the same way as the participants in my study struggled to achieve non-oppressive families. The context in which I was working, my sense of relative powerlessness (over the definition of my work as sociology, necessary if I was to be awarded a PhD) and my lack of confidence influenced to what extent and in what manner these principles were put into practice.

Finding a Sample

As the key defining characteristic of the population studied is that they are consciously political in their living arrangements,[1] I have used a volunteer sample formed by contacting various organizations and advertising in feminist media. Although the respondents needed to identify themselves as coming within the scope of the project, I had already developed my own sense of the possible range, based on both structural and relational characteristics. The research was conducted in Britain.

Although it is widely accepted that the nuclear family household with male breadwinner and female housewife is statistically a minority living arrangement, it is this view of 'family' that feminist critiques and most mainstream sociological literature addresses. Elsewhere I have documented the way that the family household consisting of heterosexual, married couple with children where the man has primary responsibility for the financial maintenance of the unit and the woman for the day-to-day emotional and physical care underpins much British social policy, an influential factor in many people's lives (VanEvery, 1992). In addition, sociological studies have documented the salience of a popular belief in this type of living arrangement as an ideal (e.g. Brannen and Moss, 1991; Kiernan, 1992, pp. 97–100).

My list of possible alternatives included living arrangements without children or with other than two adults, as well as heterosexual couples with children where the division of labour was other than male breadwinner (or primary earner) and female housewife (or primary carer of home and children). My hypothetical sample was thus divided into six groups based on two initial criteria: (1) three divisions based on the number of adults (one, two, more than two); (2) two based on the existence of children (with, without).

With the intention of covering as broad and varied a sample as possible, I contacted various organizations including the British Organization of Nonparents (BON), the Working Mothers' Association, the National Council for One Parent Families, and Gingerbread. I also advertised, initially in the December 1990/January 1991 issue of *Everywoman* magazine and the Women's Page of the *Guardian* (9 April, 1991).[2] The advertisement that appeared on the *Guardian* Women's Page was worded as follows:

> Calling all alternative lifestyles ... PhD student Joanne VanEvery is researching Anti-Sexist Alternatives to the Patriarchal Family and wants to interview people from all types of anti-sexist arrangements, including heterosexual parents who share the work, parents single by choice, voluntarily childless couples and collective households with or without kids. Write to her at the Department of Sociology ...

The exact wording was devised by the Women's Page staff based on information contained in my letter to them. The other advertisements had similar wording.

The wording of the advertisement raises the issue of definition. 'Family' is a term that is popularly understood. Even if respondents did not call their living arrangement a family, they would be able to relate it to one. I must stress that the adjectives used in the advertisement were of equal stature to or greater importance than the nouns. Thus it was not just 'alternatives' to the 'family' that I was studying (perhaps necessitating some clear definition of each) but *'anti-sexist* alternatives' to the *'patriarchal* family'. The focus was very much on the anti-sexist character of the living arrangements studied.

I used the term 'anti-sexist' instead of 'feminist' largely because of debates about the definition of the latter term and a recognition of the reluctance of some women to describe themselves as feminists.[3] The use of the term 'patriarchal' was not meant in the narrow sense often used to describe a particular historical form of the family but rather in the broader sense of the term as used within late twentieth-century feminist discourse. As Jackie Stacey puts it:

Originally used to describe the power of the father as head of household, the term 'patriarchy' has been used within post-1960s feminism to refer to the systematic organization of male supremacy and female subordination.

(Stacey, 1993, p. 53)

She points out that, despite academic disagreements about the use of the term, it has an important symbolic status in feminist activism. It is as a political rather than theoretical term that I have used it here.[4] There is no way of knowing from the information collected what respondents understood by the term or even whether there was any uniformity to their understandings.

The response to the call for participants varied. BON responded by sending a list of people that I could contact for interviews. The Working Mothers' Association put a notice in their newsletter. I have had no response from the other organizations. The response was large enough at this stage to construct a reasonably varied interview group of a size suitable for the time available to complete the project. I made no further attempts to find possible participants.

I compiled a list of 62 respondents including seven who responded to the advertisement in *Everywoman*; two who responded to the notice in the Working Mothers' Association newsletter; 48 who responded to the advertisement in the *Guardian*; one whom I met at a conference entitled 'Men, Masculinity and Socialism'; and four who were referred by other respondents whether in an interview or in the initial response. The list does not include people referred from BON, one respondent to the *Everywoman* advertisement, one respondent to the *Guardian* advertisement, or six who were referred by other respondents.[5]

Who Responded?

Many of the respondents wrote with quite a lot of detail thus permitting me to choose whom to interview based on a range of factors including type of arrangement, geographical location, length of relationship, age, occupation and income.[6] Age and length of arrangement varies. One couple wrote while still expecting their first child; two of the single parents have children over 20. A few respondents mentioned having lived in another type of alternative arrangement previous to the one they are currently in.

The geographical distribution was as follows. There were 18 respondents from London plus three from Kent and one from Surrey which could be grouped together as South East. In the North West there were four from

Manchester, and one each from Wigan and Liverpool; in the North, five from Sheffield, Hebden Bridge, Leeds and York. In East Anglia there were two respondents from Cambridge, and one each from Norwich, Northampton, St Albans, Luton and Royston (Herts). In the Midlands there were three each from Birmingham and Nottingham, and one each from Coventry and Leicester. Two respondents were from south-east Scotland. One was from the Northeast (Co. Durham). In the South and South West two respondents were from Bristol, and one each from Cardiff, Holsworthy (Devon), Brighton, Portsmouth, Oxford and Waterlooville (Hants).

Although useful sociological tools, categories are never as clear cut as they seem. My categories changed once I had real cases to put into them, but they are still inadequate in many ways. They are also still useful, primarily in sorting out the pros and cons of various arrangements. Is it because of the way the relationship is arranged that certain options become (im)possible? Or are people constrained to arrange their personal lives in particular ways? What effect does the arrangement have on the distribution of power? Or can any arrangement be anti-sexist if the will is there?

My initial categorization, based on number of adults and the existence/ lack of children, did not take a couple of important points into consideration. The first was sexuality. On the original criteria, the lesbian couple with children would have been lumped in with all the other couples with children. I now feel that, although I may want to compare their situation to those of heterosexual couples, their sexuality makes a significant difference both to the way they arrange their lives and the constraints that they face.

Sexuality is also important in differentiating relationships containing the same number of adults. One woman's situation illustrates this. Although a single parent by choice, she had, on more than one occasion, shared a house with one other woman in an arrangement where they shared housework and the care of their collective children. However, this was not a couple relationship. The issue of sexuality and the status of couple becomes important in categorizing these arrangements. Similarly some of the multiple adult arrangements contained couples and others didn't. This appears to make a difference to the situation of the individual women involved. These issues are still not fully addressed by the revised categories but I have problematized them in the analysis.

The second issue that my original categorization didn't address was the many ways that a couple relationship might be arranged. This is what led me to split the role-reversal situations from those with shared roles. The criterion here is whether the division between paid work outside the home and voluntary work, housework and child-care is challenged or not. In the role-reversal situation it is not, although the gendering of that division is; in the shared-role situations it is. However, this is not as clear a division as it might appear. Sometimes the decision to arrange a role-reversal situation was pragmatic — the option of shared roles was not available. There was also one couple in the shared-role category who had originally planned a role reversal but the woman opted for work satisfaction over higher pay thus necessitating employment for both of them.

The new categorization tried to accommodate these issues and resulted in six categories: single mothers by choice,[7] voluntarily childless heterosexual couples, heterosexual couples with children in role-reversal situations, heterosexual couples with children with shared roles, multiple adult arrangements and 'others'. The list of 62 respondents can be broken down into seven single mothers by choice, 10 voluntarily childless heterosexual couples, 10 heterosexual couples with children in role-reversal situations, 17 heterosexual couples with children with shared roles, nine multiple adult households (including three collectives) and seven others (including a lesbian couple with children, voluntarily childless single women, and couples who do not share the same household).

Limitations of the Sample

One of the consequences of my choice of media, and possibly the whole framing of the project, was that the distribution of respondents along the axes identified is limited. I assume most of the respondents are white.[8] The class composition is difficult to specify. Using an occupational indicator, the majority of the respondents are in what might be termed middle-class occupations (e.g. teaching, social work, community work, self-employed). However, many of those interviewed report coming from working-class backgrounds. Looking at income most would still probably be classified as middle class, although there is quite a lot of variation: from reliance on state benefits to over £200000 per annum. Most are well educated, many having university degrees (some postgraduate degrees) or other post-secondary qualifications.

Only one respondent mentioned in a letter not being heterosexual although a couple of women have said they question the validity of sexual identity as a categorization (don't identify either way). This has important implications for the analysis of couples. Patriarchy affects heterosexual couples in a different way than it affects lesbian or gay couples. There is a problem, however, with characterizing all of my respondents as heterosexual. The single mothers by choice are not in the same relationship to men as women in heterosexual couples even if they identify as heterosexual (see

Frye, 1992). Of those interviewed, one of the single mothers now identifies as a lesbian; one does not identify herself either way; and one is primarily celibate although she identifies as heterosexual. The one lesbian couple was included in the 'other' group and heterosexuality was problematized in the analysis. This led me to focus on the strategies of heterosexual women in the book. The lesbian couple appear only where their situation clarifies a point.

The apparent white, middle-class bias of the sample is at least partly due to the nature of the question. It has been argued that the importance of the family as a political issue varies with class and 'race'. Issues of survival may take precedence, or different cultural norms (e.g. the prevalence and acceptance of female-headed households in the Afro-Caribbean community) may diminish the importance of struggle in this area. These are difficult issues which have been debated in the feminist literature for some time (e.g. hooks, 1984). I would argue that the normative model of the family is implicitly a white middle-class one. Black and working-class women *may* be struggling against some aspects of that norm simply by keeping their own traditions.

Many women have other reasons for not living in some alternative to the normative family. As Barrett and McIntosh have pointed out (1982, pp. 147–8) pursuing alternative living arrangements requires either a willingness to 'put up with considerable material privation' or personal resources in excess of those available to poor women. This was confirmed by my research: most of the people I interviewed could have been earning considerably more if their commitment were not so strong; and they could live relatively comfortably on this 'lower' income. Many black women are in the lower income strata of British society as are working-class women. They do not have the same choices regarding working hours that middle-class people do. This effectively limits the number of women who are not white and middle class in the population from which I have drawn my sample.

I considered advertising in other publications and areas, for example gay and lesbian magazines and newspapers, other women's movement magazines and newspapers,[9] women's centres, and lesbian and gay centres. Because of the size of the project I have decided not to do this. If the types of arrangement were too varied by sexuality, race and class then a sample of 25–30 could have been no more than a set of case studies. Although four or five similar situations do not allow for broad generalizations they at least give some indications in that direction which one could not glean from one, perhaps idiosyncratic, case.

There are also benefits to a sample limited in these ways. The project is in part an evaluation of a certain type of 'personal' politics — is it possible to change the gender relations within our own living arrangements? The privileges that white, middle-class heterosexuals have make them the most likely to be able to effect change in their personal lives. They are not constrained by poverty, racism or disability, thus the constraints specific to the social organization of the family are more clearly discernible. Much research on changing gender relations has focused on the changing economic situation in working-class communities. The results of this research have been disappointing for those expecting a challenge to traditional gender roles (see Morris, 1990). Perhaps those studies were looking for change in the places it was least likely to occur. For example, they have commonly been studies of male manual workers for whom job loss was a challenge to gender identity which prompted a reassertion of familiar values (e.g. Morris, 1985; Bell and McKee, 1985). However, even where high-earning, well-educated samples have been used, economic change was not sufficient to change gendered roles (Hertz, 1986).

In addition the research is, at least in part, not about the people themselves but rather about the structures and processes beyond their control which affect their ability to live in the way that they would like. Dorothy Smith addresses the issue of representativeness in her more recent work.

> Taking the standpoint of women means relying on women's experience. This is what I've done here. There's no sample, no attempt to generalize in the ordinary sense. I do not argue that the few instances I avail myself of are representative or typical. I'm proceeding in a different way, from the assumption that any such story bears ineluctable traces of the social organizations and relations that are integral to the sequences of action it retails.
>
> (Smith, 1990, p. 217, fn 33)

However, in so far as I am trying to determine what sorts of alternatives exist and how they work, it is useful for me to have a broad and varied sample and to try to determine whether patterns are discernible, if only in small groups of similar arrangements.

Deciding Who to Interview

The distribution of those interviewed tried to allow for comparison of similar arrangements to avoid the problem of idiosyncratic cases while also allowing me to demonstrate the diversity of arrangements actually existing. Choices were made on two primary criteria: that the respondents be distributed across the categories of arrangement; and that there be geographical variety.

Of the 62 replies, I conducted 28 interviews, two of which were rejected as unsuitable (see note 4). In the analysis I used material from interviews with four single parents by choice, five voluntarily childless heterosexual couples, five heterosexual couples with children in role-reversal situations, four heterosexual couples with children with shared roles, five multiple adult arrangements and three others. I also used the information in two of the letters that I received. The shift of focus for the book has meant a main group of 25 living arrangements. The lesbian couple has been removed from the 'other' category and now provides additional information. Many of the respondents spoke about previous living arrangements or seemed to straddle two categories. When necessary, the analysis will take this into account and include information from other categories to supplement discussion. A brief description of each living arrangement is given in Appendix 1.

Of the other axes of distribution geography was the most important. Geographical distribution has been clustered for practical/financial reasons.[10] Geographically, the sample was distributed as follows: six from London and three from the South East, two from the South West, three from the West Midlands, three from the East Midlands, three from East Anglia, one from the South Coast, three from the North West, and two from south-east Scotland.

Interviewing Techniques

Most of the interviews took place in the summer of 1991, though a few were in the spring or autumn of that year. The interviews were semi-structured and informal and usually took place in the homes of the respondents except for a few cases where they were conducted in public places (i.e. pub, restaurant, workplace). Members of living arrangements were interviewed once as a group. I had made a decision not to interview children. Otherwise who was presented for the interview was determined by the respondents. The interviews usually lasted between 60 and 90 minutes although in a few cases they were longer. The interview was recorded on cassette. I also took some written notes. In preparation for interviewing I constructed a list of 11 topics that I wanted to cover with possible questions under each topic. The topics were: (1) general information, (2) attitudes and ideas about child-care and mothering, (3) work, (4) child-care, (5) school, (6) relationships both within the household unit and with others who live elsewhere, (7) state support, (8) money, (9) division of labour in the home, (10) politics and (11) feelings about space (public and private). I usually started by describing briefly the purpose of my research and asking them to describe their living arrangement to me. It was necessary in some cases to ask a lot of questions, in others I made minimal interventions. The interview technique seemed to depend on the personalities of the respondents. Those who were used to discussing their relationship either amongst themselves or with others gave much more information. Those who were generally more reserved needed more prompting and gave briefer answers.

The different character of various interviews might be explicable in terms of the respondents' ability to transform their everyday experience into a form comprehensible in the context of my research. Dorothy Smith (1990) points out that the concepts used in professional discourses construe reality in a particular way. Thus validity becomes an issue of where one is placed in the hierarchy and the power to define that this position implies:

> ... systematic approaches to questioning such as those used in psychiatry or in the structured interviews of sociological methodologies predigest primary narrative so that it is already construed as documents to the discursive schema.
>
> (Smith, 1990, p. 194)

By using unstructured interviews I was avoiding this prestructuring of my respondents' reality to a certain extent but I was still responsible for choosing what was relevant to my question both during and after the actual interview. Marjorie DeVault (1990) points out that the language with which to describe our daily practices may not be available. Thus women may rely on the interviewer having a shared understanding in order to convey the details that she seeks.

The interview material was analysed using an interpretive method. The small size of the project allowed me to immerse myself in the interview material without the assistance of computer packages. Basically, the analysis involved reading and rereading the detailed interview notes to determine important themes. Then, when working on particular themes, more systematic collation of relevant information from the interviews was carried out. I did not code and separate sections of the interviews reading only relevant sections for each topic (although I did write numerous notes in the margins). For each theme I reread the entire interview distilling the information gradually as the analysis progressed. During this process I realized that information I had originally thought related to one topic was useful for others. Because of this I feel that the ability to deal with whole interviews is an advantage of the small-scale project.

Distance and Feedback

I often found that the respondents wanted some feedback from me regarding the research during the interview. Often this was information about what other respondents were doing. Sometimes it was about the uses of the research. I tried to let them speak about their arrangements unprompted at first but would then raise issues from other interviews for comment if I thought that they might be important. More detailed discussion of some of the information was usually at the end of the interview.

In one case the respondents asked for more detailed information before the interview so that they could think about it and therefore use the time more efficiently. Although I had reservations about this regarding the value of what they would tell me, it seemed to work rather well. By giving this one couple more detailed information before the interview I allowed them to decide what was relevant. This has traditionally been considered a problem in socio-logical research which necessitates the intervention of the researcher to evaluate the truthfulness of the information gained. I would argue that it is in fact consistent with the feminist position outlined above in that it reduces the sociologist's role to one of using her analytical skills and access to other information.

The difficulty of escaping traditional ideas of objectivity in research was made clear. Although I had researched feminist methodology prior to conducting the interviews I still felt nervous about giving too much information about the project at the beginning of the interview. This problem arose particularly when I felt that another participant's experience might provide a solution to a problem that the interviewee was having. The exchange of information from other interviews was not the only difficulty. There were also occasions where something that the interviewee said tapped a problem (or solution) in my own relationship which I wanted to discuss. I am conscious of suppressing that urge in order to 'do the research'. Despite my recognition of the role that my personal life played in the formulation of the question, and implicitly in the analysis, I was unwilling or unable to deal explicitly with my personal experiences in the context of the research. Although critical of the traditional role of the sociologist I was unable to breach the 'distance' requirement to the extent that my life could become an organizing principle of the research.

I have tried to give the participants some feedback since the interviews. This has been difficult owing to the way that I write.[11] They have been given the opportunity to comment on some of the material.[12] Some of their comments have been incorporated. I have also used additional information provided in letters by some participants. Although I specifically asked for comments, I also feel that one purpose of this procedure is to give them information both about what I am doing with the information that they gave me and about how others in the study are organizing their lives. Problems of distance and expertise are not limited to the researcher. Despite asking for comments on the analysis most participants were reluctant to make more than factual corrections. Clearly the location of the researcher in the relations of ruling (to use Dorothy Smith's phrase) structures this relationship and feminist researchers will need to address this actively if more egalitarian research methods are to be possible.

Notes

1   They are political in the sense that their motivation has something to do with bettering the position of women in society.
2   *Everywoman* is a monthly feminist magazine; the *Guardian*, a national newspaper with a left liberal orientation. Its women's page is considered to be feminist and a common anti-feminist slur is to call someone a '*Guardian* Women's Page reader'.
3   Indeed some of the participants did not call themselves feminists. There is also a debate about whether men can be feminists which might have affected the response.
4   For a summary of the theoretical debates see Stacey (1993, pp. 52–9). For arguments in support of its use in a broad descriptive sense to denote the power relationship between men and women in society, see Gittens (1993, pp. 35–6).
5   Although self-definition as falling within the scope of the project was considered sufficient, I did exclude several people who wrote to me, or whose names were supplied to me. The reasons for their exclusion are given here.

    I interviewed one of the people referred by the British Organization of Nonparents (BON) and it was apparent that she was a representative of the organization and not particularly suitable for the research. Since some of the others referred by BON have appeared in newspaper articles about the organization, I assumed that they also would be representing the organization.

    The only respondent to the *Everywoman* advertisement who was excluded was also interviewed. Although her living arrangement is clearly unconventional, it is not anti-sexist (this was confirmed by the respondent in the interview).

    The respondent to the *Guardian* advertisement who was excluded is a single father (widower) whose letter implied that his arrangement was not consciously anti-sexist. I had no response to my letter requesting him to confirm whether or not he should be included.

    The others have not responded in their own right and therefore have not been included although they would have been considered for interviews if necessary. I have included some living arrangements despite being referred by others for specific reasons to do with their particular arrangements.
6   There were a few who stated only that they were willing to be interviewed. I asked them for further details and have received these in two cases.
7   I originally called this category 'single parents by choice' but as all the respondents

who fit into it were women I have changed the name. Presumably gender affects the experience of single parenthood.

8   This assumption was based mostly on names (no one has identified themselves by 'race' in their letter) and has been supported in the interviews (chosen for location and type of arrangement) where all have been white.

9   It was suggested to me that had I advertised in *Spare Rib*, a feminist magazine (no longer in existence) which had a record of covering Black feminist issues, I might have had a less 'white' response.

10 I tried to choose cities where there were multiple respondents, especially if they were at some distance from Colchester (where I was living at the time). Near the end of the interviewing I did travel for single interviews but these were within a reasonable distance. I would have liked to allow for urban/rural distribution as well but, considering my dependence on public transportation, this was not possible.

11 I have tried to complete rough drafts of everything before editing and amending any first drafts.

12 I sent copies of a conference paper to the three participants whose stories I had used in it asking them for comments. All three responded briefly and their comments have been taken into account in later stages of the analysis. I also sent a report containing that conference paper (modified) along with a publication arising from the research to all the participants. When the analysis of the interview material for the three main chapters was complete I sent a copy of those three chapters (before the major editing) along with an outline of the thesis and a draft of the participants' descriptions (used above) to all the participants (except one whose first package of material was returned undelivered).

References

ABRAMS, P. and McCULLOCH, A. (1976) 'Men, women, and communes' in BARKER, D.L. and ALLEN, S. (Eds) *Sexual Divisions and Society: Process and Change*, London: Tavistock Publications.

ACKER, J. (1990) 'Hierarchies, jobs, bodies: a theory of gendered organizations', *Gender & Society*, **4**, 2, pp. 139–58.

BACKETT, K. (1982) *Mothers and Fathers: A Study of the Development and Negotiation of Parental Behaviour*, London: Macmillan.

BACKETT, K. (1987) 'The negotiation of fatherhood', in LEWIS and O'BRIEN (Eds) op. cit., pp. 74–90.

BAKER, E. L. (1993) 'For richer, for poorer, in your name or in mine', *The Guardian*, 2 June, p. 13.

BANKS, O. (1981) *Faces of Feminism: A Study of Feminism as a Social Movement*, Oxford: Basil Blackwell.

BARRETT, M. and McINTOSH, M. (1982) *The Anti-Social Family*, London: Verso.

BEECHEY, V. (1987) *Unequal Work*, London: Verso.

BEECHEY, V. (1988) 'Rethinking the definition of work: gender and work' in JENSON *et al.* (Eds) *Feminization of the Labour Force: Paradoxes and Promises*, Cambridge: Polity.

BEECHEY, V. and PERKINS, T. (1985) 'Conceptualizing part-time work' in ROBERTS, B. *et al.* (Eds) *New Approaches to Economic Life*, Manchester: Manchester University Press.

BELL, C. and McKEE, L. (1985) 'Marital and family relations in times of male unemployment' in ROBERTS, B., FINNEGAN, R. and GALLIE, D. (Eds) *New Approaches to Economic Life*, Manchester: Manchester University Press, pp. 387–99.

BELL, N. W. and VOGEL, E. F. (Eds) (1960) *A Modern Introduction to The Family*, London: Routledge & Kegan Paul.

BENSTON, M. (1969) 'The political economy of women's liberation', *Monthly Review*, September.

BERK, S. F. (1985) *The Gender Factory: The Apportionment of Work in American Households*, London: Plenum Press.

BLUMSTEIN, P. and SCHWARTZ, P. (1983) *American Couples*, New York: William Morrow.

BRANNEN, J. and MOSS, P. (1988) *New Mothers at Work: Employment and Childcare*, London: Unwin.

BRANNEN, J. and MOSS, P. (1991) *Managing Mothers: Dual Earner Households After Maternity Leave*, London: Unwin Hyman.

BURGOYNE, C. B. (1990) 'Money in marriage: how patterns of allocation both reflect and conceal power', *Sociological Review*, **38**, pp. 634–65.

BURGOYNE, J. (1991) 'Does the ring make any difference? Couples and the private face of a public relationship in post-war Britain', in CLARK, D. (Ed.) *Marriage, Domestic Life and Social Change*, London: Routledge.

CENTRAL STATISTICAL OFFICE (1992) *Family Spending: A Report on the 1991 Family Expenditure Survey*, London: HMSO.

CHANDLER, J. (1991) *Women Without Husbands: An Exploration of the Margins of Marriage*, London: Macmillan.

CHARLES, N. and KERR, M. (1988) *Women, Food and Families*, Manchester: Manchester University Press.

CHEAL, D. (1991) *Family and the State of Theory*, Toronto: University of Toronto Press.

CHODOROW, N. (1978) *The Reproduction of Mothering: Psychoanalysis and the Sociology of Gender*, Berkeley: University of California Press.

COCK, J. (1981) 'Disposable nannies: domestic servants in the political economy of South Africa', *Review of African Political Economy*, **21**, pp. 63–83.

COCKBURN, C. (1991) *In the Way of Women: Men's Resistance to Sex Equality in Organizations*, London: Macmillan.

COLEMAN, M. T. and WALTERS, J. M. (1989) 'Beyond sex role explanations: the division of household labor in gay and lesbian households', paper presented at the American Sociological Association Conference.

COLTRANE, S. (1989) 'Household labor and the routine production of gender', *Social Problems*, **36**, 5, pp. 473–90.

COOPER, J. (1991) 'Births outside marriage: recent trends and associated demographic and social changes', *Population Trends*, **63**, pp. 8–18.

COVERMAN, S. (1985) 'Explaining husbands' participation in domestic labor', *Sociological Quarterly*, **26**, 1, pp. 81–97.

COWAN, R. S. (1989) *More Work for Mother: the Ironies of Household Technologies from the Open Hearth to the Microwave*, London: Free Association.

DELPHY, C. (1977) *The Main Enemy*, Women's Research and Resources Centre Publication: Explorations in Feminism No. 3.

DELPHY, C. (1992) 'Mothers' union?', *Trouble & Strife*, **24**, pp. 12–19.

DELPHY, C. and LEONARD, D. (1992) *Familiar Exploitation: A New Analysis of Marriage in Contemporary Western Societies*, Cambridge: Polity Press.

DESAULNIERS, S. (1991) 'The organization of housework in lesbian households', unpublished paper presented at the Canadian Women's Studies Association annual conference, Kingston, Ontario.

DEVAULT, M. (1990) 'Talking and listening from women's standpoint: feminist strategies for interviewing and analysis', *Social Problems*, **37**, 1, pp. 96–116.

DORNBUSCH, S. M. and STROBER, M. H. (Eds) (1988) *Feminism, Children, and the New Families*, London: Guildford Press.

DOWRICK, S. and GRUNDBERG, S. (Eds) (1980) *Why Children?* London: Women's Press.

DUNN, N. (1977) *Different Drummers*, London: Lorrimer.

EICHLER, M. (1988) *NonSexist Research Methods*, London: Unwin.

EISENSTEIN, H. (1991) *Gender Shock: Practising Feminism on Two Continents*, Sydney: Allen & Unwin.

ELLIOT, F. R. (1986) *The Family: Change or Continuity?* London: Macmillan.

FEE, E. (1988) 'Critiques of modern science: the relationship of feminism to other radical epistemologies', in BLEIER, R. (Ed.) *Feminist Approaches to Science*, New York: Pergamon Press, pp. 42–56.

FINCH, J. (1983) *Married to the Job: Wives' Incorporation into Men's Work*, London: Allen & Unwin.

FINCH, J. (1989) *Family Obligation and Social Change*, Cambridge: Polity Press.

FRIEDAN, B. (1963) *The Feminine Mystique*, London: Gollancz.

FRYE, M. (1983a) 'Sexism', in *The Politics of Reality: Essays in Feminist Theory*, Trumansburg, NY: Crossing Press, pp. 17–40.

FRYE, M. (1983b) 'On being white: thinking toward a feminist understanding of race and race supremacy', in *The Politics of Reality*, op. cit., pp. 110–27.

FRYE, M. (1983c) 'Some reflections on separatism and power', in *The Politics of Reality*, op. cit., pp. 95–109.

FRYE, M. (1992) 'Willful virgin or do you have to be a lesbian to be a feminist?' in *Willful Virgin: Essays in Feminism*, Freedom, CA: Crossing Press, pp. 124–37 (originally published 1990).

GAITSKELL, D., KIMBLE, J., MACONACHIE, M. and UNTERHALTER, E. (1984) 'Class, race and gender: domestic workers in South Africa', *Review of African Political Economy*, **27/28**, pp. 86–108.

GELSTHORPE, L. and MORRIS, A. (Eds) (1990) *Feminist Perspectives in Criminology*, Milton Keynes: Open University Press.

GERSHUNY, J. (1983) *Social Innovation and the Division of Labour*, Oxford: Oxford University Press.

GERSHUNY, J. I. *et al.* (1986) 'Preliminary analysis of the 1983/84 ESRC time budget data', *Quarterly Journal of Social Affairs*, **2**, pp. 13–39.

GILMAN, C. P. (1979) *Herland*, London: Women's Press (originally published 1915).

GITTENS, D. (1993) *The Family in Question*, 2nd edn, London: Macmillan.

GORDON, T. (1994) *Single Women: On the Margins?* London: Macmillan.

GRAHAM, H. (1982) 'Coping: or how mothers are seen and not heard', in FRIEDMAN, S. and SARAH, E. (Eds) *On the Problem of Men: Two Feminist Conferences*, London: Women's Press, pp. 101–16.

GREGSON, N. and LOWE, M. (1993) 'Renegotiating the domestic division of labour? A study of dual career households in north east and south east England', *Sociological Review*, **41**, 3, pp. 475–505.

HARDING, S. (1987) 'Introduction: is there a feminist method?' in HARDING, S. (Ed.) *Feminism and Methodology*, Milton Keynes: Open University Press, pp. 1–14.

HARRIS, C.C. (1983) *The Family and Industrial Society*, London: George Allen & Unwin.

HERTZ, R. (1986) *More Equal Than Others: Women and Men in Dual-Career Marriages*, Berkeley: University of California Press.

HERTZ, R. (1992) 'Financial affairs: money and authority in American dual earner marriage', in LEWIS, S. *et al.* (Eds) *Dual-Earner Families: International Perspectives*, London: Sage, pp. 127–50.

HIMMELWEIT, S. (1988) 'More than "A Woman's Right to Choose"?', *Feminist Review*, **29**, pp. 38–56.

HOCHSCHILD, A. (1983) *The Managed Heart: The Commercialization of Human Feeling*, Berkeley: University of California Press.

HOCHSCHILD, A. (1989) *The Second Shift: Working Parents and the Revolution at Home*, London: Piatkus.

HOCHSCHILD, A. (1990) 'Ideology and emotion management: a perspective and path for future research', in KEMPER, T.D. (Ed.) *Research Agendas in the Sociology of Emotions*, Albany: State University of New York Press, pp. 117–42.

HOMER, M., LEONARD, A. and TAYLOR, P. (1985) 'The burden of dependency', in JOHNSON, N. (Ed.) *Marital Violence*, London: Routledge & Kegan Paul, pp. 77–92.

HOOKS, B (1984) *Feminist Theory: from Margin to Centre*, Boston, MA: South End Press.

JACKSON, S. (1992) 'Towards a historical sociology of housework: a materialist feminist analysis', *Women's Studies International Forum*, **15**, 2, pp. 153–72.

JEFFREYS, S. (1985) *The Spinster and Her Enemies: Feminism and Sexuality 1880–1930*, London: Pandora.

JOHNSON, M. (1988) *Strong Mothers, Weak Wives: The Search for Gender Equality*, Berkeley: University of California Press.

JOHNSON, M. (1989) 'Feminism and the theories of Talcott Parsons', in WALLACE, R. A. (Ed.) *Feminism and Sociological Theory*, London: Sage, pp. 101–18.

JOWELL, R., WITHERSPOON, S. and BROOK, L. (1987) *British Social Attitudes: the 1987 Report*, London: Social and Community Planning Research.

KALUZYNSKA, E. (1980) 'Wiping the floor with theory — a survey of writings on housework', *Feminist Review*, **6**, pp. 27–54.

KIERNAN, K. (1992) 'Men and women at work and at home', in JOWELL, R. *et al*. (Eds) *British Social Attitudes: The 9th Report*, Aldershot: Dartmouth.

LEONARDO, M. DI (1987) 'The female world of cards and holidays: women, families and the work of kinship', *Signs*, **12**, 4, pp. 440–53.

LEWIS, C. and O'BRIEN, M. (Eds) (1987a) *Reassessing Fatherhood: New Observations on Fathers and the Modern Family*, London: Sage.

LEWIS, C. and O'BRIEN, M. (1987b) 'Constraints on fathers: research, theory and clinical practice', in LEWIS and O'BRIEN (Eds) op. cit., pp. 1–19.

LOPATA, H Z. and THORNE, B. (1978) 'On the term "sex roles"', *Signs*, **3**, pp. 718–21.

MACKLIN, E. D. (1980) 'Nontraditional family forms: a decade of research', *Journal of Marriage and the Family*, **42**, 4, pp. 905–22.

MANSFIELD, P. and COLLARD, J. (1988) *The Beginning of the Rest of Your Life: A Portrait of Newly-Wed Marriage*, London: Macmillan.

McCULLOCH, A. (1982) 'Alternative households', in RAPOPORT, R. N. *et al.*, *Families in Britain*, London: Routledge & Kegan Paul.

MILLETT, K. (1971) *Sexual Politics*, London: Hart-Davis.

MOLYNEUX, M. (1979) 'Beyond the domestic labour debate', *New Left Review*, **116**, pp. 3–27.

MORGAN, D. H. J. (1992) *Discovering Men*, London: Routledge.

MORRIS, L. (1985) 'Renegotiation of the domestic division of labour', in ROBERTS, B. *et al.* (Eds) *New Approaches to Economic Life*, Manchester: Manchester University Press.

MORRIS, L. (1989) 'Household strategies: the individual, the collectivity and the labour market — the case of married couples', *Work, Employment and Society*, **3**, 4, pp. 447–64.

MORRIS, L. (1990) *The Workings of the Household: A US–UK Comparison*, Cambridge: Polity Press.

Moss, P. and Brannen, J. (1987) 'Fathers and employment', in Lewis and O'Brien (Eds) op. cit., pp. 36–53.

Nava, M. (1983) 'From Utopian to scientific feminism? Early feminist critiques of the family', in Segal, L., *What is to be Done about the Family?* Harmondsworth: Penguin, pp. 65–105.

Oakley, A. (1974a) *The Sociology of Housework*, London: Robertson.

Oakley, A. (1974b) *Housewife*, London: Penguin.

O'Brien, M. (forthcoming) 'Allocation of resources in households: childhood perspectives', *Sociological Review*.

Pahl, J. (1980) 'Patterns of money management within marriage', *Journal of Social Policy*, **9**, 3, pp. 313–35.

Pahl, J. (1983) 'The allocation of money and the structuring of inequality within marriage', *Sociological Review*, **31**, pp. 237–62.

Pahl, J. (1985) *Private Violence and Public Policy*, London: Routledge & Kegan Paul.

Pahl, J. (1989) *Money and Marriage*, Basingstoke: Macmillan.

Pahl, R. E. (1984) *Divisions of Labour*, Oxford: Blackwell.

Pahl, R. E. (1988) *On Work*, Oxford: Blackwell.

Parsons, T. and Bales, R. (1955) *Family, Socialization and Interaction Process*, Glencoe, IL: Free Press.

Parsons, T. and Smelser, N. J. (1956) *Economy and Society: A Study in the Integration of Economic and Social Theory*, London: Routledge & Kegan Paul.

Pateman, C. (1983) 'Feminist critiques of the public/private dichotomy', in Benn, S. I. and Gaus, G. F. (Eds) *Public and Private in Social Life*, Beckenham: Croom Helm.

Pateman, C. (1988) *The Sexual Contract*, Cambridge: Polity Press.

Peace, H. F. (1993) 'The pretended family — a study of the division of domestic labour in lesbian families', *Leicester University Discussion Papers in Sociology*, S93/3.

Peterson, S. R. (1984) 'Against "parenting"', in Trebilcot, J. (Ed.) *Mothering: Essays in Feminist Theory*, Totawa, NJ: Rowman and Allanheld.

Pitrou, A. (1978) *Vivre Sans Famille?*, Toulouse: Privat.

Pleck, J. (1985) *Working Wives/Working Husbands*, Beverly Hills, CA: Sage.

Polatnick, M. R. (1984) 'Why men don't rear children: a power analysis', in Trebilcot, J. (Ed.) *Mothering: Essays in Feminist Theory*, Totawa, NJ: Rowman and Allanheld.

Popenoe, D. (1988) *Disturbing the Nest: Family Change and Decline in Modern Societies*, New York: Aldine de Gruyter.

Raymond, J. (1991) *A Passion for Friends: Towards a Philosophy of Female Affection*, London: Women's Press (originally published 1986).

Rich, A. (1977) *Of Woman Born: Motherhood as Experience and Institution*, London: Virago.

Richardson, D. (1993) *Women, Motherhood and Childrearing*, London: Macmillan.

Rowbotham, S. (1972) 'Women's liberation and the new politics', in Wandor, M. (Ed.) *The Body Politic*, London: Stage I.

Rowbotham, S. (1989a) *The Past is Before Us: Feminism in Action Since the 1960s*, London: Pandora.

Rowbotham, S. (1989b) 'To be or not to be: the dilemmas of mothering', *Feminist Review*, **31**, pp. 82–93.

Russell, G. (1987) 'Problems in role-reversed families', in Lewis, C. and O'Brien, M. (Eds) *Reassessing Fatherhood*, London: Sage.

Sang, B. (1984) 'Lesbian relationships: a struggle toward partner equality', in Darty, T.

and POTTER, S. (Eds) *Women-Identified Women*, Palo Alto, CA: Mayfield.

SEGAL, L. (Ed.) (1983) *What is to be Done About the Family?* Harmondsworth: Penguin.

SMART, C. (1984) *The Ties that Bind: Law, Marriage and the Reproduction of Patriarchal Relations*, London: Routledge.

SMITH, D. (1988) *The Everyday World as Problematic*, Milton Keynes: Open University Press.

SMITH, D. (1990) *The Conceptual Practices of Power: A Feminist Sociology of Knowledge*, Toronto: University of Toronto Press.

SNITOW, A. (1992) 'Feminism and motherhood: an American reading', *Feminist Review*, **40**, pp. 32–51.

STACEY, J. (1993) 'Untangling feminist theory', in RICHARDSON, D. and ROBINSON, V. (Eds) *Introducing Women's Studies*, London: Macmillan.

STACEY, J. and THORNE, B. (1985) 'The missing feminist revolution in sociology', *Social Problems*, **32**, 4, pp. 301–16.

STAMP, P. (1985) 'Balance of financial power in marriage: an exploratory study of breadwinning wives', *Sociological Review*, **33**, pp. 546–57.

STANLEY, L. and WISE, S. (1983) *Breaking Out: Feminist Consciousness and Feminist Research*, London: Routledge & Kegan Paul.

STANWORTH, M. (Ed.) (1987) *Reproductive Technologies: Gender, Motherhood and Medicine*, Cambridge: Polity Press.

STATHAM, J. (1986) *Non-Sexist Child Raising*, London: Blackwell.

SYDIE, R. A. (1987) *Natural Women, Cultural Men: A Feminist Perspective on Sociological Theory*, Milton Keynes: Open University Press.

THOMAS, G. and ZMROCZEK, C. (1985) 'Household technology: the "liberation" of women from the home?', in CLOSE, P. and COLLINS, R. (Eds) *Family and Economy in Modern Society*, London: Macmillan.

THORNE, B. (1987) 'Revisioning women and social change: where are the children?' *Gender & Society*, **1**, 1, pp. 85–109.

Trouble & Strife (1993) Special issue 'Radical feminism in the 1990s', *Trouble & Strife*, **27**.

TUTTLE, L. (1986) *Encyclopedia of Feminism*, London: Longman.

UNITED NATIONS (1991) *The World's Women 1970–1990: Trends and Statistics*, New York: United Nations.

VANEVERY, J. (1992) 'Who is "the family"? The assumptions of British social policy', *Critical Social Policy*, **33**, pp. 62–75.

VOGLER, C. and PAHL, J. (1993) 'Social and economic change and the organisation of money within marriage', *Work, Employment and Society*, **7**, 1, pp. 71–95.

VOGLER, C. and PAHL, J. (1994) 'Money, power and inequality within marriage', *Sociological Review*, **42**, 2, pp. 263–88.

WARING, M. (1989) *If Women Counted: A New Feminist Economics*, London: Macmillan.

WEEKS, J. (1991) 'Pretended family relationships', in CLARK, D. (Ed.) *Marriage, Domestic Life and Social Change*, London: Routledge.

WEST, C. and ZIMMERMAN, D. H. (1987) 'Doing gender', *Gender & Society*, **1**, 2, pp. 125–51.

WITHERSPOON, S. and PRIOR, G. (1991) 'Working mothers: free to choose?' in JOWELL, R. *et al.* (Eds) *British Social Attitudes: The 8th Report*, Aldershot: Dartmouth.

WITZ, A. (1993) 'Women at work', in RICHARDSON, D. and ROBINSON, V. (Eds)

Introducing Women's Studies, London: Macmillan.

WRIGHT, E. O. *et al.* (1992) 'The non-effects of class on the gender division of labor in the home: a comparative study of Sweden and the United States', *Gender & Society*, **6**, 2, pp. 252–82.

YOUNG, M, and WILMOTT, P. (1973) *The Symmetrical Family*, London: Routledge & Kegan Paul.

Index